DUOver™ Praises

"The Matchmaking DUO, Kelli Fisher and Tana Gilmore, have remained authentic and have always had a heart for helping people through coaching and matchmaking. They continually seek additional knowledge and raise the bar by staying abreast of the latest trends and approaches in the industry. We are so proud of the launch of their new book. It is a true testament to their desire to help others and spread love which is the most valuable treasure anyone can have."

Lisa Clampitt
President and Co-Founder
The Matchmaking Institute
New York, NY

"Kelli Fisher and Tana Gilmore of The Matchmaking DUO are highly sought after for their advice and coaching on love and relationships. I applaud them for devoting their lives to helping amazing women and men find true love through their professional expertise and experiences. Congratulations on the book ladies!"

Charli Penn
Relationship Expert
Founder of ManWifeandDog.com

CONTENTS

AUTHOR'S NOTE

ALL identifying details of third party scenarios have been changed to protect the privacy of individuals. Names, places, and events are used in a fictitious manner for explanation only. Any resemblance to actual persons, living or dead, or actual events is purely coincidental.

To women all across the world of different ages and stages of dating and relationships. You deserve a DUOver™ to embrace your new role as a loving and supportive other half in a committed relationship. Regardless of how many times you've tried in the past, never give up on finding love again. Dust yourself off armed with new information to boost your confidence and prepare you, so this time will be your last!

ACKNOWLEDGMENTS

KELLI

FIRST, I thank God for always being with me through the ups and downs of life, a true roller coaster. But that ride and all of my experiences, good and not so good, delivered me to my purpose and divine destiny. There's not too much any of my clients can throw at me that I have not lived and overcome. What an awesome plan. Looking back all I can say is, "Thank you Lord!"

To my family, the wind beneath my wings, Thank you! My mom, Terri Fisher, who is the perfect blend of business woman, cheerleader, listener, woman of God, fashion stylist, and one who provides never-ending love. My dad, Dr. Harold Fisher, a true family man, provider, supporter, and man of faith who is always in my corner no matter what darts come my way. A marriage of almost 50+ years, wow such an accomplishment! My awesome sister, Nicole Alston, my best friend who is always there. Thank you for running this race called life with me. Sometimes we sprint, sometimes it's long distance but always together and for that I am so grateful. My brother-in-law, Paul Alston, who has been a constant in my life always offering the stability I needed from afar and showing me dependability and love through his actions. My aunt, Willa Blackshear, the glue that holds our family together; always offering a warm smile, a listening ear, and an encouraging word. I doubt there are too many people on this earth more giving than you. And to my grandparents: Rosalie Blackshear, a true gem of beauty, wisdom, and laughter at 90+ years young (I will age well) and Oscar and Augusta Fisher, who also lived together until their 90's but left with me their love of family, deep-rooted faith, and showed me that so much can be accomplished from little to nothing. It's not where you start but where you end.

To my beautiful daughters, Nia, Nyla, and Nyelle, and my lovely niece Autumn, who fuel my fire each and every day to do more, to be more, and to share more in hopes that they will find true happiness in their authenticity. May you learn from my missteps to arrive better, stronger, and confident in who you are, who you need, and all that you will offer. I love you!

To all of the Pastors who have helped me form my own spiritual journey of faith; The late Rev. Oliver Brown, Rev. Doris Glaspy, Rev. Dr. Craig P. Riley, Pastor Emma Salter, Pastor De'Andre Salter and Lady Terri Salter, Pastors Earl and Sophia McBride, and Rev. Dr. Michael and Rev. Twanna Henderson. Your wisdom and guidance have strengthened my relationship with God and you have shown me a glimpse of His immeasurable love for me through your support, insight, and willingness to follow Him as I followed you, thank you! To the infinite number of family, friends, church families, and business and spiritual mentors; each one of you is so important and I would be crushed if I forgot someone so I will say thank you to all. I love each of you for every ounce you have poured into me. My prayer is that God returns it to you 100 fold, exceedingly, abundantly, and above all you could ever ask or think.

To Tana's husband, Trey Gilmore, I must thank you for how you stepped in and supported me with my daughters after my leap of faith move to North Carolina. I never even considered you in my initial plan but God provided a "ram in the bush" and you truly lived out the words you would continually tell me, "It takes a village."

Finally to my partner in crime and co-author, Tana Gilmore, there are not enough words to say how much your friendship has meant to me throughout the years. We met in business almost 15 years ago but have been there for each other through so much more…there's no way we could fit it all in one book! Thank you for being such a wonderful friend, business partner, Sorority sister, confidante, prayer partner and voice of reason all rolled into one. What a blessing! I'm so thankful we're in this together and I look forward to continuing this journey for many years to come.

Love, Kelli

TANA

I would like to thank God for trusting me to deliver a message to His children. I thank Him for believing in me and arming me with the life experience and the gift of connecting with people even when I doubted myself.

To my late Granny Marie McIntosh, thank you for being the epitome of strength and setting the example of a matriarch. For that I am now carrying the torch. To my late Granny Sarah Dove, thank you for depositing and planting the seed of Jesus in me at an early age. I would not be the bold prayer warrior I am today if it were not for you. To my late grandmother-in-law Ella Gilmore, I used to love the stories you would share of you and daddy Gilmore and how you took care of him until he transitioned. I strive to emulate your love as a wife.

I thank my husband Trey Gilmore for being "Team Tana" every

day, all day. Thank you for allowing me to live out my dreams, your love and support is unbridled. I'm so blessed to be your wife and couldn't have done this without you. I love you to life! To my mom Geneva Passley, you have taught me how to be strong and successful yet humble. From a very young age, your sacrifices to give me a better life are appreciated more than you'll ever know. YOU are the ultimate "giver." To my fathers Garry Simpson and Sam Gibson, thank you for setting the example of what I should look for in a great husband (I found him). To my mother-in-law Olivia Gilmore and late father-in-law Exter Gilmore Jr. , thank you for raising a great son and allowing me to see what a marriage is supposed to look like. To my Aunt Geraldine Milam, you have been a mentor and role model my entire life and I will forever look up to you. My Uncle Sean McIntosh, no words can describe how much I love you.

To my children TJ Dent, Torree Fair, Candyce Gilmore, Quay Gilmore and Quiera Gilmore. I love you and I am so proud of each and every one of you. I pray I have set an example that all things are possible if you work hard and believe it! To Yasemin Kaftanci, thank you for being a great mom to my first grandson(s) Dominic and (Luca bonus grandchild). They are the wind beneath my wings. To my siblings, Tamara Simpson, Dr. Venita Simpson, Melissa Simpson, Nadya Simpson, Sintoria Matthews, Tephanie Gibson, Marcell Milam and Tevin Simpson, my special niece Tieara Smith, family and dear friends, I love each every one of you and thank you for your love and support.

To my Bishop Herbert C. Crump and Freedom Temple Ministries Family, words cannot express the spiritual guidance and deliverance that has taken place in my life since 2008 when I joined this church. My spiritual maturity and boldness is a result of learned behavior. I thank God for you. Special thanks to Mother Sandra Thompson and

Minister JaVonda Ellison, Minister Bry-anne Jones and the Freedom Temple Intercessory Prayer Team. You have prayed with me and for me for the last 7 years with us meeting on the prayer line at 5AM every morning. I thank you!

Finally, to my "ride or die" Kelli Fisher, co-author, friend, business partner, Soror and faith-walking partner, you are Thelma and I am Louise. Never in a million years 15 years ago would I have thought we would be here today. I'm loving God's plan. I love you!

Love, Tana

MEET THE MATCHMAKING DUO™

FOR more than a decade, "The Matchmaking DUO" have been great friends. They met while working together in Corporate America as Vice Presidents of Business Development for partnering firms. As the DUO was paired together to present to executives and entrepreneurs, their unique dual approach proved to be very successful in connecting with and retaining clients.

Throughout years of traveling across the country together on a weekly basis, the DUO endured many personal and professional challenges. Those profound experiences highlighted the alignment in their beliefs, morals, and values and revealed that they were just as successful in supporting and coaching others as they were in the boardroom – the perfect foundation for a dynamic partnership.

Kelli and Tana embrace their differences and attribute much of their award-winning success to the duality in their approach to business and life. Both Kelli and Tana are Certified Relationship Coaches and Certified Matchmakers.

Kelli

You Might Not Have Guessed: Growing up I was an accomplished violinist. I even played at Carnegie Hall and performed in a concert tour in Poland, which was amazing!

My Guilty Pleasures: Hot chocolate, chai tea, warm gourmet cookies, great shoes, and dazzling earrings.

How I Create Balance: I'm never too busy for a massage or a trip to the beach, where the water is turquoise blue (I can feel the sand in my toes already)!

Tana

You Might Not Have Guessed: I love to travel and I've visited 38 of the 50 United States and a host of international destinations.

My Guilty Pleasures: Fresh baked cookies, vanilla ice cream, and watching late night television dramas or reading a juicy novel.

How I Create Balance: I've become an avid runner, running over 21 races; I completed my second half marathon (that's 13.1 miles). I love hiking and sports, primarily football—Go Steelers!

INTRODUCTION

HOW many times have you said to yourself, *If only someone would have handed me a manual or guide so to speak of what to do in dating and relationships.* That's how we felt. Rewind. In the beginning, we were great friends and executive colleagues traveling for weeks on end but our marriages were falling apart. We weren't in a position to quit our jobs and focus on our marriages so we cried on each other's shoulders, prayed and tried to take care of our relationships, children and homes as best we could. During that process we both ended up separated from our husbands and our children were acting out.

We thought we were doing everything right; cooking lavish meals for our families to last for the entire week while we were gone, making great money to contribute to our households, and ensuring that our kids had everything they needed for school and at home. We kept up our appearance by getting our hair and nails done regularly, dressing to impress, and wearing shoes to die for! Oh, and we had sex with our husbands when we weren't too worn out. What more could a man want, right? Let's start with quality time and encouragement, among many other things we later discovered. By the time we realized this, we were separated from our husbands. Our initial reaction was, "The nerve of him!" Yet as time progressed, we learned that it wasn't all their fault.

Now, with more time under our belt, we shared with each other all of our many failed relationships that led to failed marriages and figured out why. We realized that we had so much in common and that so many women were dealing with the same issues. All of our prayers and fasting led to a "Come to Jesus" moment, and we clearly saw the error of our ways. We recognized our Alpha female behaviors and other issues that led us to our individual DUOver™ paths. Whether we want to admit it or not, there are always two sides to every story and usually some fault on both parties even if it's not 50/50. Fast forward, since we both have a heart to help, we embarked on the road to become certified heart-hunters to assist and inform other women in making their own DUOvers™ to look forward to solid, loving and committed relationships. Countless people have commented on our transformations and our individual journey to happiness and wanted "in" on our secret.

Well here it is! The Matchmaking DUO's secret is presented in this useful guide to prevent you from making some of the many mistakes we made and adds useful learning tips along the way. Are you ready to reinvent yourself and show everyone the new and improved you? Then let The Matchmaking DUO™ walk with you step-by-step to a successful, long-lasting relationship.

CHAPTER ONE

YOUR INITIAL DUOVER™

SELF-CHECK

"Know yourself. Don't accept your dog's admiration
as conclusive evidence that you are wonderful."

-**Ann Landers**

WE'VE discovered that the first thing you should do before entering into a new relationship is to conduct an honest self-assessment of the *real* you. It is impossible to have healthy relationships if you don't have a clue as to who you are or what you want in life. Go ahead and initiate the phone calls to arrange a long overdue meeting with family or close friends. Receiving constructive criticism from third parties will only jump-start your process. Afterwards, take a minute to step back and evaluate their comments about the *real* you based on how you are perceived, so that you no longer waste valuable time making bad decisions. Many of us have spent years just "winging it" and reacting to whatever comes our way rather than creating a plan for achieving the life we desire: career, marriage, and family. Embracing self-direction provides you with a roadmap to change. It will help you become more effective and productive in everything you do.

Just like water is your body's most important nutrient, knowing yourself is equally critical to your overall mental and physical well-being. Once you take self-awareness seriously, you will be able to clearly define your purpose and goals. This is no time to get defensive because it is valuable intelligence you can use as the platform or foundation for the new you. Find a quiet place where you can put your feet up, relax and write down your answers to the following:

- What are my strengths? What do I do well in a relationship?

- What are my weaknesses? What are the top three things I need to work on?

- What are my likes and dislikes (what puts me in a good mood/a bad mood)?

- What types of people do I like to be around? Why?

- What do I really want people to know about me? Why?

- What types of environments do I enjoy? Why?

It's fairly easy for people to write down their strengths. Our "strong" characteristics are something we all want to talk about. However, it's only natural for us to omit or not own up to our weaknesses fearing they might make us seem incompetent or undesirable. Let's face it, some of us have no idea what our true weaknesses are. The downside is that if you only focus on your strengths, it's unlikely you will ever change. Just because you view certain aspects of your personality as positive doesn't mean others see them that way. Acknowledging and accepting your weaknesses is actually a great strength because it is the only way you can grow and really change. By embarking on a self-knowledge journey and being as transparent as possible, you will be more positive about your future and work diligently to achieve your goals. Being confident, having a great outlook on life, and finishing the day strong, are marketable characteristics that will make you attractive in your professional and romantic relationships.

"If you want more, you have to require more of yourself."

- Dr. Phil

Knowing who you are and what qualities are important to you are the keys to finding your mate and sustaining a long-term relationship. It takes an honest, thoughtful, and concentrated effort of reevaluating your current and past relationships to fine tune your search for *Mr. Right*. You should have your ultimate "list" of what you're looking for and if you don't, now is the time to make one. Yet how many times have you compromised your list? Better yet, how many times did you think you found your soul mate, only to later realize that he was actually *soul bait*-a mere decoy of who you thought he was?

As you've probably seen by now, both men and women tend to put their best foot forward in the early stages of dating. As you stroll hand-in-hand during the romantic stage floating on the clouds, nothing matters except who will feed the other the last chocolate covered strawberry. Then, as time passes and you realize that it's not such a *Lovely Day* that Bill Withers sings about or you're not as *Happy* as Pharrell Williams, you begin to see your *one true love* with all of his flaws exposed. Now, the veil has been lifted, hopefully before you say "I do" and you're kicking yourself trying to figure out what you saw in him in the first place. You're not alone. Take comfort in knowing that the romantic love phase wears out quickly with the wrong person, and he has actually done you a favor. So it's back to the drawing board, but this time you will do things a bit differently since you're wiser, more focused, and ready to begin the next chapter of your life.

It's OK to feel a bit unsteady, but there is no cause for alarm because this time around you're going to create your DUOver™ list and stick to it! Make your list the deal-breaker that it needs to be so you clearly see the errors in your previous decision-making that led you to choose the last guy. Then wipe the slate clean. Stop asking yourself, *Was it me? Was it him?* Quit focusing on the time you wasted. Either way, something did not gel between the two of you, and chances are you were blind-sided by the red flags. Unfortunately, for several wrong reasons like, *I don't want to be alone,* or *he's not as bad as John,* or *I can change him,* you hung in there when the yellow dead-end sign was in plain view.

YOUR DUOver™ CHECKLIST:

√ **Character** - Does he do the right thing when no one is watching?

√ **Integrity** - Do his words mirror his actions so that everything he says matches what he does? Do you have full access to him any time of the day or night?

√ **Financial Wisdom** - Is he good with his finances? Does he have good credit?

√ **Decision-making** - Can you trust him to make decisions on your behalf? Can he lead you? Is he resourceful and has problem-solving skills to creatively find solutions?

√ **Respect** - Does his family and peers respect him? Does he respect senior citizens and children (which will show his compassionate side)?

√ **"Grindability"** - Will he get out and grind and work hard when times get tough?

√ **Morals** - Do the values and the religious beliefs he talks about align with his actions? What is his level of priority when it comes to family, marriage, children, step-children? Did he have any successful marriages around him and how did those marriages operate?

TAKE IT FROM ME

When I was younger I wanted "The Most Attractive Man on Earth." I later learned that a man wearing that title on his forehead came with a high price—a price that meant I was constantly competing with other women. I felt like I was under a lot of pressure in those relationships trying to look exceptional at all times and be the best at everything.

Now I tell women that the average looking guy will think you're a beauty queen and wear you like a badge of honor. Over time he will become *better* looking than Idris Elba or George Clooney in your eyes. I advise women to look for a man who is smart with an amazing personality, supportive, makes you laugh and can push you beyond your comfort zone. What we see time and time again as coaches is that he may not be your first choice initially, but go on a date two or three times with a man who exhibits these qualities and you may be pleasantly surprised. Additionally, look for a guy that knows how to pray for you when you can't muster up a prayer. All of these qualities will help you sustain a long-lasting, loving relationship.

ARE WE COMPATIBLE?

"To be happy with a man you must understand him
a lot and love him a little. To be happy with a woman
you must love her a lot and not try to understand her at all."

- Helen Rowland

We often get asked compatibility questions like, "How do I know if I am compatible with someone? Is chemistry important in the beginning? Is it true that opposites attract?" We don't look at compatibility as an all or nothing factor. Instead we believe there are degrees of compatibility that should be taken into account. Keep in mind that compatibility is a lot more than just getting along with your mate. It's knowing that he has compatible values and qualities on your DUOver™ list, which should be issues that are equally important to you. Take time to consider core values that you share or those where you are clearly polar opposites. Chances are, if there were never any *core* values that you had in common, you're incompatibility would lead to a break up anyway. Therefore, the sooner you evaluate your personality and your DUOver™ deal-breakers, the more likely you will have success in finding that ideal person. You must be brutally honest with yourself and your new mate as to what makes you tick, get ticked off, and makes you happy.

Having some type of chemistry with the guy you're considering entering into a relationship with is great because *at least* it means you are attracted to him. When you get those butterflies in your stomach at the sight of him or feel genuinely happy just being around him, that chemistry will allow you to get to know him more because you will work to spend more quality time together. Just keep in mind that chemistry is not just an exterior quality. It can be developed over time with actions like him taking the lead, making you feel safe or having great conversations that continue for hours on end. Retrain your mind to expand your limits on what you define as chemistry and give it some time even if his looks are not 100 percent your "type." You will eventually discover true compatibility trumps "easy on the eye" and will foster that long-lasting relationship you are looking for.

One final note, if you already know you are inflexible, then you are not going to get along with another inflexible mate. Two people cannot both always be right. Being inflexible is detrimental in your relationship as arguments will arise frequently from the stress and frustration of one person thinking he is perfect and right all the time.

TAKE IT FROM ME

Early on, I had very little parameters and was more concerned about looks, a great body, great conversation, a general feeling of exclusivity and a guy who was a foodie like me! I didn't place much value on education level or earning power. In my first marriage, I had no idea what it meant to be a wife. My first husband was 12 years older than me. When we met I was making great money, had my own house, drove a sports car, and my kitchen was spotless because I ate take-out every day. During the dating phase he cooked every meal. I was pretty immature and knew nothing about being a wife. Eating and traveling were the premise of our relationship. We often dropped everything and hit the open road or an airport to discover new destinations together. Then we decided to get married. The dining out and traveling came to an abrupt halt as we started this new life together. It was like, "Kelli, you're a wife now, and you need to kick it into wifey gear!" I never acted in a serious wife role before, nor had we discussed finances or responsibilities like cooking or cleaning. I wasn't sure if we were supposed to have a traditional marriage or was it 50/50? What were our goals in life and how were we going to get there together? I had no idea. I was so immature and busy having a great time dating that I never tackled the real issues that needed to sustain the relationship. Sound like anyone you know? I'm sure. Yes, I drove a cute sports car and knew how to shift gears, but this new arrangement was a total shock to my system. Needless to say my marriage lasted eight months. The good news is that we eventually had a chance to talk as friends and settle our differences.

TAKE IT FROM ME

In my 20's when I was single and dating I discovered that I gave too much of myself to demonstrate that I was wife material and catered to my guy's every need. I lost my identity and self-esteem in the process. By giving away everything I realized it didn't make me any more wife material than the "man on the moon," as my grandmother Marie often said. "Why buy the cow when you can get the milk for free?" was another one of her favorites. I gave him nothing to look forward to in the future. I later learned that it was all in my posture and confidence. I didn't have to prove to him or anyone else of my self-worth. It had to resonate with me first. Needless to say when I was giving all of myself out of fear of breaking up or sheer desperation, the relationship ended anyway. Always asking myself *Why?* and *What if?*, while he quickly moved on to the next woman and married her!

***

The fact is, in a lot of relationships, people initially send their representative of who they want you to see. It seems impossible to be totally compatible with a person and then totally incompatible a few weeks or months later. There is no point in pretending to be someone that you are not because your true self will eventually appear whether or not you want it to. Therefore, compatibility is great if the two of you are presenting a non-photoshopped picture of the real you. With so many types of compatibility tests available online today, have fun with them and take a few variations to test your consistency. Be sure to check out our **TandemMatch**™ which closely evaluates your personal needs and lifestyles in order to create your **TandemID**™ personality assessment. Again knowing your DUOver™ deal-breakers along with an honest personality assessment will put you well on your way to finding the *One*.

THE SOUL MATE DEBATE

Soulmate
Until the end of time
You're my soulmate
I'll love you till I get to heaven's gate
And if I go first sweetheart
I'll wait
'Cause I know I'll never find another
Soulmate...

- Josh Turner and John David Anderson

We believe that there is a special person for everyone of you out there. Since none of us is perfect, there is a "perfectly imperfect" match for you. In our office we don't use the term "soul mate." The notion that there is only one human being in the entire universe who is the best compliment to you is just a fairy tale. The only One who can complete you is God. However, He desires for you to be in relationship with each other in order to learn, grow, experience and show love. The soul mate debate will always be a heated topic, yet we will not dwell on it because at the end of the day, sitting around waiting for your soul mate is the equivalent of waiting on your Boaz to appear at your door and never leaving the house.

The key here is to keep your eyes open and continuously work on your spiritual foundation. The person who may be "perfectly imperfect" for you could be right under your nose, standing in your predestined path. Connecting with someone is not just about a magical feeling when you see him or her. Yes, birds chirping and butterflies in your stomach are great, but there has to be more than just *feelings*. Don't settle for trusting your emotions because they can be fickle, and when times get tough those warm and fuzzy feelings fade and usually leave one person or both hurt. Seeking a healthy relationship with your "perfectly imperfect" person should be based on several items on your DUOver™ Checklist.

When you meet a guy and you can effectively communicate, understand each other, and have a few things in common that's a wonderful start. There should also be some level of intellectual complement so that you both have a good understanding of life's challenges and work together to solve issues as they arise. As you get to know him better and you both are interested in moving forward, there will be an emotional give-and-take which tells the other person what you're willing to compromise on which can lead to happiness. So during this phase you will quickly see where you both stand. Are you giving and he's not budging? Is he giving and you're not too moved? The goal should be that you are both all-in.

SELF-ASSESSMENT DUOver™ TIPS:

- Take your self-assessment seriously. Enlist as many people whom you trust to provide constructive feedback. Knowing who you are and what you want in life are the keys to sustainable growth, love, enjoyment and peace.

- Put your trust in the facts— not just your emotions. If his actions show you that your new mate is a liar, unfaithful, or has a bad reputation, then that is who he is regardless of the sales pitch. Accept the reality that this is the real person you are seeing today. No one is perfect, so weigh the pros and cons to determine whether this is a workable relationship for you in the long-term.

CHAPTER TWO

YOUR FORGIVENESS DUOVER™

"The only way to create a more loving, productive, and fulfilling life is by forgiving the past. Releasing the past restores us to the full energy of the present moment."

- Iyanla Vanzant

FORGIVENESS is one of the hardest emotional and behavioral actions that we are capable of expressing. It takes great courage and strength to forgive. For one thing, it shows the other person and onlookers that you are not out for revenge. Second, it demonstrates that all anger and bitterness toward that person are really gone. When you forgive you are releasing better opportunities for yourself which will free you from the bondage of carrying grudge-fueled excess baggage. We have found that true forgiveness is when you can still maintain a genuinely amicable relationship with a person that has done you terribly wrong. If you have children, think of the excellent role model you can be to your son or daughter if they see you getting along with your ex when that child knows some of the things each of you did to hurt the other. Showing maturity, unity, and a pure heart despite the circumstances is likely to make that child similarly forgive others or even forgive you in the future if God forbid, you make a mistake as we all have done at some point.

"True forgiveness is when you can say thank you for that experience."

- Oprah Winfrey

We've learned over time, and you may have too, that every experience in life whether good or not so great contributes to the person you are today. Many life coaches and psychologists describe forgiveness as a "practice." That means that you have to work at it often, if not daily. Take time to practice these forgiveness DUOver™ Tips below.

FORGIVENESS DUOVER™ TIPS:

- Purchase a journal to record and acknowledge your hurt and emotions.

- Have a serious conversation with the person to tell them how you feel while also clearly letting him or her know that you forgive them. If they are no longer around you can call or mail a letter. If they have passed away, still write everything that you wanted them to know and shred it.

- If thoughts of hurt continue to upset you, meditate more and try to engage in activities that help you relieve stress, i.e. working out, Yoga, or taking a morning or afternoon walk.

- Pray for forgiveness, pray for the person who hurt you, when you grow tired of praying, pray some more.

"In life when you empty the trash the new will begin to pour into you, but you have to forgive and truly forget about it and move on."

- Bishop Herbert C. Crump

Think about all those times you've said to someone, "I'll forgive you, but I won't forget what you did." Forgiving is a great first step, however, *forgetting* is the really hard part. If you hold on to your past incidents with a person by not forgetting, you will forever be held hostage by the situation. Bishop Crump of Freedom Temple Ministries preached a sermon on forgiveness and shared a story of how he called his cable company because he was not receiving emails. The customer service representative told him that he had too many emails and that he needed to log into his account and delete as many emails as possible. He spent two hours deleting emails. To his surprise he still had not received *one* email. He called the cable company back and they said, "Well sir there is one more step you need to take." "What else do I need to do?" he replied. "You have to empty the trash." As soon as he emptied the trash hundreds of new emails immediately came in. He used this same analogy to tell the congregation that in life when you empty the trash, the new will pour into you, but in order for that to happen you have to forgive *and* forget about it or you will be stuck longer than necessary. Of course we realize it's easier said than done, but with practice, patience and a spiritual foundation, you will be on your way to true healing and true forgiveness—like Jesus desires for us. Granted, we are not God, but He will forgive us of our sins and remembers them no more (Is. 43:25).

Now that you've forgiven the person for past hurt, it's time to wipe the slate clean, move on and forget it. This means that you have to erase it from your mind's hard drive. Continue living your life knowing that you have learned from the experience and are in a position to help others with similar experiences along the way.

TAKE IT FROM ME

After my divorce I realized I was still harboring a lot of unforgiveness. *Why me?* I relived the role of the victim over and over in my mind. But it wasn't until I truly forgave my now ex, as well as myself, that I felt totally free and mentally available to receive a new relationship. I knew that I arrived when I could hold my head up high, smile and genuinely wish him well.

***

As we have said, the *forgetting* part is really tough. Instead of dwelling on what your ex did, try to reestablish your faith and focus more on God and not your predicament. Ask Him to empty your heart to rid you from past hurts. We've spoken to a lot of women and they have spent too much time being mad at their ex and voicing to others, "Can you believe what he did to me?" Many of them did not realize that it was heavy baggage weighing them down. Once you get to the point where you can forgive and release it from your spirit you can move on and be better prepared spiritually and emotionally. For those of you who are married or still in a relationship, sometimes you will need the extra help of the person who hurt you to help you heal and forget. So if your spouse cheated and you chose to forgive him, it is his responsibility to help restore the trust in the relationship. We tell men to start doing this by checking in often, providing more information than necessary about their day, and spending more quality time with their significant other.

MEET JENNIFER

Most women have some type of past baggage from previous relationships. Whether infidelity, emotional, mental or physical abuse, it's difficult to move forward into a new relationship without revisiting the past hurt. Infidelity ranks high amongst failed marriages or couple break-ups. When the cheating happened more than once, it's only natural for a woman to have a tough time trusting the same man again.

Jennifer was in an unhealthy relationship for over six years. Her man cheated on her throughout the relationship which ultimately resulted in another woman becoming pregnant. Each time he cheated, the apologies seemed more sincere than the last. Jennifer invested so much into this relationship that she was determined not to throw in the towel. Year-after-year, blow-up after blow-up, she still held on to hope that he would one day propose. In her mind, she was doing everything that a wife would do which led her to believe she was totally wife material. *Why couldn't he see that?* He finally broke it off and married another woman!

> *Jennifer:* You know, I spent so many years hating him for what he did to me. I would say things to myself like, *The nerve, who does he think is? How could he do this to me? After all I did for him?*

> *Kelli:* What was the turning point for you?

> *Jennifer:* After a few years of literally agonizing over this, one day I woke up and it hit me like a ton of bricks. Everything that happened to me I let happen. I was his doormat and he knew it. No matter what he did I was going to take him back. And to think I still wanted to marry him after

a child and a lot more cheating. I realized that he did me the biggest favor of my life. He was never right for me in the first place. I totally see that his walking out like that, as cold and hurtful as it was, was the best thing he had ever done for me.

Tana: You know, that's really your blessing.

Jennifer: Yes, I know. So now instead of hating him, I forgive him for all that he put me through. I have also forgiven myself because I wasted so much time blaming myself for his actions. I let it go and now I am ready to do this the right way. The man of my dreams is out there and I am going to find him—with your help of course!

JENNIFER'S DUOVER™

Trust was a huge issue for Jennifer. She compared every man to her former cheater. Anytime a guy had to cancel on her or was running late, she accused him of lying and cheating. She found herself spending countless hours trying to decipher email and cell phone passwords to investigate the truth for herself. It was eating her up inside. We stressed the importance of allowing new people to have a clean slate through forgiveness, owning up to her contributions, and allowing herself to believe in love again. In Jennifer's case, one of the most critical take-aways was self-evaluation.

Self Evaluation - We asked Jennifer to make a list of what she learned from that relationship and what she needed to let go. Everything happens for a reason and there were some things she learned about herself that were very positive which she could capitalize on. We also wanted her to carefully consider what type of role she wanted to have in her relationships going forward.

DUOver™ FORGIVENESS AWARENESS TIP:

- Start with a clean canvas.

- You cannot forgive without forgetting. You will know you have released the incident from your spirit when you can think about the person or engage in activities with the one who hurt you as though it never happened. It is detrimental to your well-being to continue referencing the pain or bringing baggage from past relationships into a new one.

- If you are still in a relationship and have elected to forgive, make sure you have an "end date" to release yourself and the person from the incident. Especially if he is doing all he can to win your trust again. Don't hold the hurt over his head forever. If you do, you're missing out on the freedom and peace of living a life of true forgiveness.

TAKE IT FROM ME

It took me over 20 years to realize that I was operating in error because I was forgiving but *never* forgetting. That's why it's important for me to speak to men and women and inform them that if they told their mate that they have forgiven them for past cheating or lying about a major incident, then let it go! I advise them that it's not fair to the other person to keep holding it over their head month-after-month or year-after-year every time a disagreement arises. If you have truly forgiven you have to move on and forget about it. It's a hard thing to do. It took me a while, but I can now say that forgiveness is my goal. Once I made my forgiveness request known in the atmosphere it began to slowly creep into my spirit and it has become genuine. God has totally released me from past hurts which let's me know that I have grown more spiritually mature. Now that I am in this comfortable place of peace I actually feel free. I'm on a mission to help others get to this point.

CHAPTER THREE

"OVER & OUT"

"When men and women are able to respect and accept
their differences then love has a chance to blossom."

- Dr. John Gray

He said: Babe, do you know why Adam was created first?

She said: No, I wasn't at that meeting!

He said: To give him a chance to say something!

LET'S face it, men and women communicate differently. Effective communication is the key to any sustainable relationship. In fact, Dr. John Gray expressed these differences when he concluded that men and women are from different planets in his international bestseller, *Men Are From Mars, Women Are From Venus.* Miscommunication between men and women is quite common. Each one is looking for a response from the other that is gender-related. Men expect women to respond in a male communication style, while women expect men to tap into a female emotionally-charged communication response. Who's right? Neither. Understanding and recognizing the differences in male-female communication styles is a special gift that keeps on giving, leaving both parties fulfilled.

TAKE IT FROM ME

During my marriage, when heated disagreements arose, on impulse I went on and on getting my point across to him. Then, I immediately called my close girlfriends and family to further regurgitate all of the details to get reassurance that he was "wrong" and I was "right." The thing that came back to bite me later was after we made up and were back in love, many of my girlfriends and family were now jaded and naturally still mad at him because of the argument. Each time I called everyone in a tizzy exposing all the details, the more their opinion of him went quickly downhill. Ladies, please know that as difficult as it may be, because we love to share, limit what you discuss with others regarding your relationship. Although you are upset at the moment, pray to God for clarity and if you must, share with someone who has shown their support for both of you and will have an unbiased opinion where they can remove their own emotions from the situation and steer you in the right direction.

MEET LESLIE

Leslie has been in a committed relationship for two years. She and her boyfriend usually get along well, however, every few months she found herself frustrated after an argument about her boyfriend's failure to communicate. She was discouraged about this issue and came to us for help.

> **Leslie:** I really didn't want to go to a counselor about this because although it's very important to me, I don't want to drag my boyfriend into someone's office to talk about our disagreements. He wouldn't be comfortable with that which would make things worse.
>
> **Tana:** Yes, most men balk at the idea of counseling initially.

Leslie: I'm hoping that you can help me learn how to get him to see that I'm a different species from him, and when I talk I'm just really trying to connect with him. I think I say the same things over and over because I just want him to get it. I'm really worried because this last time, I finally decided not to talk to him. I figure, if he doesn't want to talk why bother?

Kelli: You should always keep the lines of communication open. How does he communicate?

Leslie: Well I've noticed that he will be engaged for the first five minutes, but when our conversation gets too detailed, he checks out.

LESLIE'S DUOVER™

After several coaching sessions, Leslie discovered that her communication style was too wordy with no real plan for resolution, while her boyfriend was solution oriented. His goal when communicating was to solve the problem and move forward and hers was to make him acknowledge how they arrived. Through coaching, Leslie learned how communicate effectively in a way that she could offer a condensed version of the events but also participate in a plan to make it work.

TAKE IT FROM ME

I'm an in-your-face type of communicator! I like to address conflict and situations one-on-one as soon as they come up. However, my husband likes to write out his thoughts via email or text message. *What? Is he for real?* This wasn't working for me initially. Yet I learned to compromise. He told me that I did not give him a chance to get everything out before I had already formed my opinion on the issue. We agreed to wait to allow him to first write out his thoughts and send them to me. For my part, I would review his note thoroughly and discuss it with him face-to-face within the next 24 hours.

The saying "It Takes Two" is often used to refer to a number of things that can only be done with two people—communication being one of them. When two or more people get together to exchange information or share ideas they are communicating. Yet there is a difference between talking and communicating. If the other person never receives or understands your message then you are just merely talking and your point has fallen on deaf ears. Don't fret. There are simple verbal and nonverbal steps you can take to be an effective communicator.

Whenever you believe that you have to engage in a difficult conversation with your significant other, be extremely mindful of your tone. You know, "It's not what you say but how you say it!" The first thing you should consider is your body language, which is a form of nonverbal communication. Your body language speaks louder and clearer than anything you have to say. It's a good idea to mirror the other person's body language to make them feel comfortable. So if you are in a relaxed and open stance with your arms to your sides it will make the other party feel like they can approach you. This can be the start of a good conversation. However, if your arms are folded and you look like The Hunchback of Notre Dame, it tells the other party that you may be angry and unapproachable. It's a sign of a negative conversation to come.

The next important step is to make eye contact. When you look a person in the eye studies show it makes the other person feel like you are trustworthy. It also tells them that you respect them and are in tune to whatever they have to say, even if you don't fully agree. As a couple, a close connection can be formed just by staring into each other's eyes. If your mate never looks into your eyes during an important discussion it may be a sign that he has something to hide or it could be that he is not interested and tuned you out earlier in the conversation.

Finally, it's a good idea to reiterate your understanding of what the other person said. Imagine it as though you were talking on a two-way radio which can be a basic illustration of communication. Since women are likely doing more of the talking we are the transmitter: the sender of the message - *Over*. Men are the receivers of the information. When you send your message with too many details and illustrations they are likely considered noise which is a distraction that can take away from your point. Try to stay as direct as possible. Then there is feedback between you and your mate to ensure that you understand each other - *Roger*. After a clear understanding there is a replication that there has been a meeting of the minds - *Out*.

TAKE IT FROM ME

During my marriage when things bothered me I held my tongue to keep the peace. Eventually, every miniscule or large thing my husband did drove me absolutely crazy. Instead of telling him how I felt I picked up the phone to get my friends and family to co-sign my point of view and see him in a negative light. So technically, I never really held my tongue, I just put it on layaway! What was I thinking?

SHOW & TELL

"Men want the same thing from their underwear that they want from women: a little bit of support, and a little bit of freedom."

- Jerry Seinfeld

The more we sit down with our clients the more we realize that overall men seek commitment, support and sex!

In one of our workshops men told us that they wanted the following qualities in a woman:

1) If she is a Christian, she needs to provide more than religious conversation or activities. What kind of movies do you like? Do you like music? Do you like to travel?

2) She should be sexy and appealing to the eye, both out in public and at home. Some women are all dolled up for work and when they come home they put on sweats or a worn-out bathrobe.

3) She should provide genuine encouragement and praise both at home and in front of others. Ladies, consider the things he does great and acknowledge them often, even on social media.

4) She must get her point across quickly and be prepared to offer viable solutions. Men appreciate direct communication. Instead of complaining about a situation, have helpful advice.

5) She should be conscious of her tone—you can attract more bees with honey.

6) She proactively supports his vision and has the skillset to help him get his goals off the ground. Ladies, men appreciate it when you take on their vision for the house and for the future.

7) She is creative, spontaneous, and keeps him on his toes. Since men get bored quickly, be prepared to introduce intriguing things to do and places to visit.

8) She is discrete and keeps their affairs private. Men really

dislike when women involve their family and girlfriends into every aspect of the relationship.

DUOVER™ Workshop
The Art of Flirting

Very often female clients come to us saying they don't have the slightest clue how to flirt, but wish they did. Once they see that interested guys were right under their noses and they froze like a deer in headlights, then they realized the need for a lesson in the art of flirting. Did you know that flirting is skill? That means it can be learned and developed which is great news! Why let the opportunity to chat with a potentially great guy go to waste because of your fear of rejection. This is an important skillset that we can certainly help you conquer.

CHAPTER FOUR

YOUR DATING DUOVER™

*God only matched one couple, Adam and Eve, and when
they blew it, He got out of the matchmaking business!"*

- The Matchmaking DUO™

DO SOMETHING!

WE have to remind our clients that they will never have a date
sitting at home on the sofa Friday and Saturday nights. Even
for the most "sanctified" Christian woman who is intent on waiting
for her Boaz, the odds of him knocking on her front door out of
the blue are at best, a million to one. You'd be surprised how many
women have told us that they are waiting on God or Boaz, which-
ever comes first. Our response to them is that God requires action
on their part or you won't have a reaction! Faith without works is
dead (James 2:26). If you want to be datable, you have to do your
part by putting yourself in a position to be seen, look approachable
with a friendly smile, and offer a nice "hello."

So often many women find themselves in a very boring routine.
Going the same way home, and stopping at the same store, determined to "get the task done." Unfortunately, they don't realize that a
great guy could have been staring at them just waiting for his opportunity to "find her" but some of us are too preoccupied to notice.
If you desire a man who loves the arts and is health conscious, then
you must be front and center at a museum and belong to a co-ed
gym. Just think about it, if you want to marry a doctor, you may
want to eat lunch or dinner in a hospital cafeteria twice a week—
regardless of how bad the food tastes!

Relationships and dating have become two of the hottest topics
in mainstream media today. With social networking at an all-time

high and companies like Facebook boasting over one billion users since inception, everyone is looking for some type of human connection on a daily basis. Before the social media craze, most of us sought a friend or relative to "hook us up" with an eligible bachelor or bachelorette. According to *Online Dating Magazine*, there are more than 2,500 online dating services in the U.S. alone with nearly 1,000 new online dating services opening each year. Some of the more popular ones like Zoosk.com and Match.com generate as much as 10 million visits per month.

We haven't even included the reality TV shows exposing the most drama-ridden relationships imaginable. It seems that the success of the dysfunctional newly crowned celebrities played out on TV gives us comfort in our own dysfunctional lives. Every day we are privy to relationship woes that clearly make ours appear one thousand times better! The fact is, everyone *wants* to be in a relationship so badly that it has gotten to the point where it has become a *need*. Therefore, women find themselves settling for qualities they really dislike in a man to fit in and be "normal." For those of you that consider yourself a catch but are still single, you could probably feel the occasional whispers behind your back that something *must* be wrong with you! No, there's nothing wrong with you as we mentioned earlier; the more time you spend getting to know yourself, and putting yourself in position to be found, the better suited you will be in your next relationship.

We actually thought that the show *Married at First Sight* was well done. It uses principles similar to our business practices, but they skipped the dating process altogether, like our ancestors hundreds of years ago. In Season One, two of the three couples decided to remain married which is better than the divorce rate in the United States today. Watching these couples working through their issues showed how they were committed for the long-haul. The controlled environment gave them the support and fortitude to take their marriage more seriously rather than throwing in the towel at the first sign of trouble. The end result is that we all want to have a healthy relationship with similar interests and core values.

 **TAKE TWO**: Don't just get involved with someone to have a warm body on your arm. In order to have an effective relationship with anyone, remember to be comfortable with yourself first. If you don't like being alone and find it uncomfortable, confront it head on to find out why. Do what you must to release this excess baggage for yourself and others. In the meantime, learn how to have fun with yourself on purpose. Ask yourself, *Is this God's best for me?* If you know that it really isn't, then walk away. The last thing you need to do is settle because of your impatience.

DATING 101

"When people show you who they are the first time, believe them the first time."

- Dr. Maya Angelou

A key rule of thumb during the initial dating stages is that once you identify the warning signs, take heed to them. If you ignore them, they will only get worse and make you more frustrated and miserable as time passes. Since it is our insatiable need for companionship, we often disregard the facts and move head-first based on our emotions. Often times we are surprised when we ask our clients if they have done a simple Google search about their pending date and the response is "No." We tell clients to do their research because if they are a "normal" productive citizen, there is something on the internet that will provide insight into their personality.

STICK TO YOUR DEAL-BREAKERS

Whenever you make things too easy for your mate, he will not take you seriously. If you talked about deal-breakers in the beginning of the relationship and he side-steps every single one of them and you continue to stay with him, you're headed for disappointment and heartbreak. He cannot come and go as he pleases and treat you like one of the guys. Did you ever wonder why someone you broke up with married the next person he was dating? The problem is that you didn't set boundaries. Why should he be serious with you if he knew he didn't have to? In hindsight, you may see that your ex-love's new wife made him work for her love and affection. You, on the other hand, failed to make him respect you and your "reasonable" requirements. It's all in your delivery. You don't have to whip out an iron fist. Instead, you can be firm with a smile and not lay down arbitrary expectations. If one of your most basic deal-breakers on your checklist is broken, don't let it slide. Be mindful, stick to it, as his actions should be reciprocal to how you want to be treated.

TAKE IT FROM ME

I was the girlfriend before the wife four times! I gave so much of myself and compromised who I was that guys did not respect me. I didn't require them to do anything. I invested time and energy in grooming them to be better men. I rearranged my schedule to accommodate theirs, cooked, cleaned, and took on their family responsibilities. I really thought I was supposed to be demonstrating that I was "wife material." After all, I was determined to do things differently than what I had seen growing up. Before I knew it, each one of them was *finished* with me and had moved on to *her*. After being hit with this reality over and over, I took a good look at myself and came up with a few additional deal-breakers below that I lived by when I married my husband.

* Discover who you are and your value.

* Learn to love and respect yourself.

* Never compromise and allow yourself to be OK being second.

INFIDELITY

"More women need to hold men accountable for their infidelity. Sounding off on the mistress is useless, her loyalty was never to you"

- The Matchmaking DUO ™

Time and time again as women discover their man is cheating, they become extremely upset with the other woman. We have heard everything from doing drivebys to stake-outs, waiting around the corner to try and get a glimpse of "her," so they can jump out and show the other woman who's boss. What's puzzling is that women are quick to blame "her" and become argumentative and even destructive over something the man has clearly chosen to do. Yes, she is wrong also if she knew he was married or in a relationship. But why are you blaming her? When it comes to your relationship, she is not the problem...sorry to say ladies, it's him! He is the only one who can truly fix it. If you think you are just going to curse her out and make her stop seeing your man, you're in for a rude awakening. You can do tumbles and "show her just how crazy you can be" yet afterwards, your man and his other woman may be right back on the phone again or even worse, back together laughing and comparing stories of the day you acted like a wild woman. The bottom line is, her loyalty is not to you, it's to him. His loyalty should be to you, and if he has not made a major attempt to humbly repent for his ways and make drastic changes, he was never yours anyway.

It's never OK to cheat on your spouse. Let's face it, these days both men and women cheat. Both men and women have equal amounts of self-control, however, men appear to cheat more than women because men have a stronger sexual impulse. Men are naturally drawn to what they see. Yet the tide is turning and women are stepping out on their spouse in record numbers. One of the reasons sociologist Dr. Pepper Schwartz provides to account for the 40% increase in women admitting to cheating in the past decade is due to the changing economic earning power of women. Today, women don't have to rely on the incomes of their husbands as in the past, so they can afford the consequences of an affair. We found that for women, it is a lack of emotional comfort and connection. For men, two common reasons why they cheat are sexual boredom and lack of communication.

Today, infidelity is more than sexual hotel rendezvous. Emotional cheating is clearly on the rise due to technological advances and social networking. Nearly everyone has access to a mobile phone, tablet, computer or other web-enabled device that allows them one-click access to the world of cybersex, pornography, sexting, and flirting.

MEET JASMINE

Jasmine was a first for us. Her situation reads like the script of a daytime soap opera. She wasn't looking for new love, instead she desired our help in rekindling the love she has for her husband. Jasmine is a beautiful girl-next-door type in her late thirties; intelligent, friendly, smart, and great at many things. She married a successful man 15 years her senior who literally swept her off her feet the moment they met. Truly love at first sight. During the dating phase, he often surprised her with romantic getaways—even a trip to Paris on The Concord! He bought her uniquely cut diamonds and allowed her to choose the settings in rings, bracelets and necklaces. To top it off, George provided her with her own American Express Black Card. Jasmine and George married after a year and a half of dating.

Of course Jasmine didn't have to work, but she is college-educated and has an advanced degree in Human Resources. With her credentials and personality, she could work anywhere. George was very attentive, encouraging and everything about him was like clockwork. Then his business began losing revenue at an alarming rate. Now it was Jasmine's turn to be even more encouraging than before, but it wasn't enough and he felt his manhood as a provider was now compromised. George pushed her away time and time again, and voluntarily began sleeping in one of the four guest rooms.

Jasmine landed a six-figure job to help out, however George's rejection toward her led her to eventually become a workaholic. She took on extra projects, and helped out colleagues on other teams so that working late became her norm. She made a point of coming home when George was asleep. After four months of living together but separate, Jasmine started feeling lonely. Several guys at her office certainly had a crush on her and one day she decided to take Brian up on his offer to dinner, which led to a number of lunches, dinners and movies after work. Eventually they became sexually intimate. Brian was hooked and Jasmine still longed to be touched by her husband. Jasmine thought she was doing a good thing by choosing Brian because he really wasn't her type, so she felt confident that she could break it off easily and quickly. Brian wasn't willing to let her go.

> *Jasmine:* I've broken up with Brian three times and he insists he will not go away. I can't call the police because George will find out. I can't get too upset at work because I may get fired.

> *Kelli:* What is your situation with George now?

> *Jasmine:* Well, last month I confessed to him about my affair with Brian. He looked distraught. I was so afraid that Brian would tell him that I had to do it myself. George asked me to leave but I told him that I wasn't going anywhere. I told him how much I loved him and that I would do anything to get him back. I begged for his forgiveness. To prove my sincerity I quit my job.

> *Tana:* Have you two had a heart-to-heart since your confession?

> *Jasmine:* No not really. I've tried to arrange romantic evenings with him pulling out all the stops and he doesn't even show up. I've sent him texts and emails and no response. When we bump into each other in the house every now and then he will say "Good morning." I love George with all my

heart and I don't want to lose him. Please guys tell me what I should do.

JASMINE'S DUOVER™

As coaches we're trained not to tell clients what to do but rather help them arrive at the best solution for them. In Jasmine's case, we knew her goal was to remain married. We coached her through conversation scenarios to have with her husband. We helped her develop a list of talking points to air out the facts and guide the discussions. Unfortunately, George had already emotionally disconnected and could not get over her infidelity. With his new life and median income, he felt he could never measure up to the lifestyle he once provided for her. We supported her through her transition and now she's ready to find love again.

DUOver™ CHEATING AFTERMATH TIPS:

- It is important to move forward and not spend the rest of your life angry over the infidelity. You must have a positive view of your future and believe that you can always find love again should you decide to divorce.

- If you choose to forgive your spouse, he has to earn your love and trust back based on your ground-rules.

- Don't play the blame game or try to rationalize why your spouse cheated—it will only make you crazy.

- If a child is the outcome of the infidelity, be sure you can handle your spouse communicating and engaging in activities with the biological parent on a regular basis. Discussions with all three parties is a must. If you've decided to work it out, make sure you are comfortable with his explanations to her that the two of you are moving forward. In this way, everyone is on the same page and all of your interactions are out in the open. Keep in mind that it is not the child's fault and neither party should have any animosity toward the child who didn't ask to be here.

 **TAKE TWO**: We worked with a couple who after years of counseling and arguments, the wife often walked out with kids in tow. We tried one last time for reconciliation. The wife had enough of her husband's infidelity. She had forgiven him and taken him back more times than she cared to admit. At first we didn't think the wife was serious about leaving. Even her husband said that he thought they were having one of their typical disagreements where she stayed at a friends' house with the kids but always returned a few days later. But not this time. We really didn't want to see this couple separate but they separated and came to an agreement on divorcing. The reality is that sometimes you can try over and over again, but people don't change unless they want to, and it takes two people who are committed to make it work.

DUOver™ DATING DEAL-BREAKER TIPS:

Here are a few warning signs that should register on your radar:

- **Unresponsiveness:** He says he will do something or be somewhere and doesn't show up—no call or mention of it the next time you talk.

- **Lying Just Because:** He says he was helping a friend move and you find out he was at a football game. When he lies "just because" that is a sign that nearly everything he says or does will also be a lie. It's his natural inclination.

- **Cheating:** This one is up to you to decide, but please know if he has cheated on you once, there is a very strong possibility that he will do it again and he's just not that into you, so keep it moving!

- **His Place:** If you have been dating for over two months and he has never mentioned or invited you to his place, that is a sign he may be married or living with someone—even if it's his mother!

- **Last Man Standing** - He makes excuses about meeting his family or friends and tells you he enjoys being a loner. It's not very often that a man has absolutely no close relatives and you can be sure he will flock to them during the holidays. If you're not invited or around for those memorable events, *Houston we have a problem*!

- **Abuse** - Zero tolerance for any type of abuse: verbal, mental, emotional, or physical as it will continue throughout the relationship.

- **Insecurity/Jealousy/Possessiveness** - If you have to provide your significant other with your locator throughout the day, this is a sign that he is insecure in the relationship. It will only get worse if you do not deal with it head on.

These are just a few red flags in the beginning stages of dating that you should not ignore. Stop believing what you want to believe. As broken as your heart may feel at the moment, you will be saving yourself more heartbreak down the line. In other words, dust yourself off and cut your losses now!

WOULD YOU DATE YOU?

"One of the biggest misconceptions that a woman has is that a man has to accept her the way she is. No we don't."

- Steve Harvey

Would you date you? Take a good long look in mirror. What does your appearance say about you? Do you look fun or unapproachable? Are you too provocative? What would men think when they see you? If you're dressed seductively they may think, "She's OK being the other woman." You should know that there is a difference between having sex appeal and being provocative. A sexy woman can captivate a man with her walk, her smile, and her body language. Many women have come to us wondering why they are always the other woman. We tell them it's because they put themselves out there in a manner that sends a signal, "I'm down for anything!" On the flip side, as a corporate professional, you cannot expect to capture a man's eye in a long, dull-brown skirt suit with a pearl necklace, pearl studs, and no makeup. Every woman needs vibrant colors in her closet, a little lip gloss, and blush. There are many ways to add flash and style to turn a corporate look into a night on the town. Just about every client who walks through our door receives assistance creating a new or refreshed style. Our DUOver™ Glam Team does a fabulous job helping create your new style and wardrobe makeover.

"If you look boring, you probably are!"

- The Matchmaking DUO™

MEET LISA

When we first met Lisa we actually would not have labeled her as an introvert. She greeted us with a smile, looked into our eyes and gave a confident handshake. Lisa was pear-shaped and petite with shoulder-length golden brown hair, and dressed in a charcoal grey pants suit. Like the majority of our clients, Lisa spent several years attaining advanced degrees and was never interested in regularly hanging out with friends. Crowds, loud music, and excessive talking really bothered her. Reading and research were her passion. Learning something new every day gave her an energy that she had not found in anything else. It wasn't so much that she wanted to share what she recently learned, just having knowledge made her feel like she had an internal power over others.

As a mid-level corporate manager, Lisa spent years dodging after-work functions, and off-site team building exercises. Of course, she certainly had to attend her share as team manager, yet she described them as pure "torture" watching everyone make fools of themselves trying to impress upper management. She enjoys going to family-type comedy movies, and usually dines at home alone watching her favorite TV shows. Needless to say, Lisa had not been on a date nor had any new personal relationships in six years.

Tana: Hi Lisa, we're so glad you were able to make it in today.

Lisa: Yes, I really wanted to be here. Although I am pretty uncomfortable talking to you about my life, I know that I have to take some course of action for my own well-being. Only my family and two close friends from college really know personal things and some of my private thoughts. I've been an introvert my whole life.

Kelli: Really? You don't come off that way.

Lisa: I guess it's because it's just the two of you and I am certainly more comfortable around women than men. I have only interacted with a few men over the years, as I am mainly surrounded by women. Sometimes overhearing other women's stories of the drama and heartache in their relationships makes me thankful that I don't have to deal with that.

Tana: Every relationship has its ups and downs. The goal is to enhance the ups so that the downs dissipate quickly.

Lisa: Like I told you before, I don't even know what I want in a guy. Of course he has to be educated and earning a living without any help from me. But I cannot imagine being involved with an introvert like me, nor do I see myself with an extrovert. Is there an in-between?

Kelli: I think we all share some of the in-betweens. Most people have areas where they are more dominant and feel more comfortable but there is always at least one side where they are not as confident.

Lisa: Don't get me wrong. I really enjoy quiet time and being alone in my thoughts, but I am not lonely. I have a few close friends and I spend time with my family at least once a month as there is always some event to attend. I guess that's why I never had this sense of urgency to find a man because I really don't consider myself lonely. I just want a healthy relationship with a "normal" man.

Kelli: So Lisa, I know you work for a large company. There has to be men throughout the building when you go to lunch or interact with in other departments. No one has ever approached you?

Lisa: No, not one.

Tana: I don't see that. You are very attractive and quite shapely. I'm sure there had to be a few heads turning at some point. It may have been that they neglected to approach you.

Lisa: It's true. As you can see, I'm not as physically fit as I'd like to be. I just don't think I'm approachable. When I see a guy coming down the hall I immediately put my head down. I think it's out of nervousness. To be honest, when I walk to the elevator bank and there are a lot of guys waiting to get on, I politely step back and fidget with my purse or briefcase and wait for the next one. I've been doing it for so long I didn't realize how bad it sounds until now that I am actually saying it out loud.

LISA'S DUOVER™

Women like Lisa often have low self-esteem and don't have the confidence to believe they can be approached. To a man, she comes across as closed-off and guarded. We started out by giving her exercises to push her outside of her comfort zone. The first priority was to make eye contact with people every day. Second, she had to take a different route home, as introverts tend to be very regimented; same grocery store, same take-out, etc. Our goal was to get her to look at the totality of her day. Then we requested that she initiate conversations with three people a week. In doing so, we provided her with exercises to finish and extend conversations. She was able to conduct friendly probes into a person's hobbies, likes and dislikes in just a few minutes. In Lisa's case, we also gave her exercises to meet additional girlfriends because this will give her the opportunity to go out and extend her network of friends. We concluded with exercises to change her body language, her communication style and provided several image tips.

>
> **Step 1**: <u>Body Language</u> - Your body language is the most noticeable non-verbal communication you possess. Walking around with your head down, arms folded, or hunched shoulders signals that you are unapproachable. Be confident in your stride, hold your head up, smile, and look people in the eye. If you are sitting, be cognizant of your posture; no slouching or elbows resting on the table. If you feel boring then you probably are. Remember you are what you feel.
>
> **Step 2**: <u>Communication Style</u> - As an introvert, Lisa is not comfortable sharing anything personal with others. We coached her on how to effectively open up and share things that would be important for someone to know about her.
>
> **Step 3**: <u>Image consulting</u> - The grey pants suit was OK because it was fitted and she could wear a bright or colorful blouse. We also suggested soft layered curls and flattering makeup. Finally, we replaced her buckled-flats with three-inch heels to really give her the confidence to look men in the eye, and let them know that she could be sexy too!

LISA'S GROCERY STORE ENCOUNTERS

- She walks up to a guy picking out an avocado. We coach her to say, "Hey do you know what you're doing?" *Teasingly with a chuckle.* "Because I don't know how to pick a good one from a bad one."

- She is standing in the seafood department. We coach her to say, "Hi what kind of fish is that? How are you going to make it?" It turns out they both had a lot in common because she fished with her dad as a kid. They continue talking about different fish, preparations, swap recipes and phone numbers.

MEET MICHELLE

Michelle's nickname in high school was "Memorable Michelle." Not only was she liked by everyone, but everyone had a memorable moment that they shared with her. Michelle's energy was contagious. She is definitely the go-to girlfriend for ladies and the go-to girlfriend for guys. When she stepped into our office the connection was instant as her Chanel perfume filled the air. She was tall, slender and wore a cleavage-revealing, red Diane Von Furstenberg form-fitting dress, with her caramel Christian Louboutin strappy heels and fierce Gucci handbag. *Why was Michelle here? What could we do for her that she couldn't do for herself?* Michelle was intelligent, beautiful, athletic, friendly and a real fashionista. She even brought us Godiva's 36-piece Truffle Gift Box! What man wouldn't want to date her?

> *Michelle:* OK ladies, like I mentioned in my email, I have a real problem finding a man who wants a committed relationship. I am sick and tired of always ending up in the "friend" zone.

MICHELLE'S DUOVER™

All her life Michelle has been the popular extrovert. She comes from a family of educated, talented, outgoing people who have surrounded her since birth. She got the lead part in the school plays, captain of the cheerleading squad, and president of the National Honor Society. Michelle was an avid sports fan and knew more about strategy and stats for basketball and football than most coaches. The challenge in her relationships has been that her extrovert personality of always being the center of attention is a turnoff for a guy who may be interested in her. A potential date may think she's off limits—just too much to handle since everyone wants to talk to her and be seen with her as if she is a celebrity. Granted, a man likes a beautiful woman on his arm, but if she takes every bit of attention away from him, he may be uncomfortable and intimidated. In other words, Michelle is the Beyoncé of her city.

> *Step 1:* Tone it Down - We explained that behaving like a high-profile celebrity, talking, waving, and making grand entrances can appear to be a bit self-centered. Consider taking it down a notch. We weren't suggesting that she instantly place herself on mute, but rather she share the spotlight and let someone else shine. When we discussed past relationships through coaching, Michelle discovered that she never consciously shared the spotlight she had created with any of her former boyfriends. She never took a moment to dote on his accomplishments or to blend herself into his world or things that were important to him.

> *Step 2:* Change vocabulary - When Michelle is going out with her guy friend, she needs to make sure she is using words to let him know that she is interested in more than friendship. So instead of using words like "let's hang out," she should say, "I'd love to spend time together tomorrow." We also made recommendations that she try to initiate doing things with other couples, and we designed more buzz

words to let the guy know that she is looking for more than just being a friend.

Step 3: <u>Wardrobe Change</u> - Is there such a thing as being too sexy? She was beautiful and well dressed, but Michelle may need to tone down her sex appeal to be taken seriously. Her low cut dresses and blouses were the first thing that men saw and it was giving the impression that she was only interested in a great time.

The 90-Day Rule

Clients inquire about Steve Harvey's 90-day rule often. One woman emailed us and was pretty distraught. She was dating someone and told him on the first date that she was not having sex until 90-days. After the 90-days, she was intimate with him and he immediately became distant and stopped treating her like a girlfriend. We advised her that we support the 90-day rule as a minimum, however, we recommend that you have at least 60 hours of face-time and talk-time within that period to get to know each other. Since she made her big announcement on the first date, he probably continued having sex with whomever was available, until it was her turn in 90-days. She may have only had three, two-hour dates in 90-days which doesn't warrant intimacy or girlfriend status. At the end of the day, men need to earn intimacy. If you haven't spent quality time getting to know him then you should hold off.

If you are experiencing a similar 90-day dilemma, step back and look at your interactions with your mate. Is he taking you on dates during that time? Does he respond to your calls? Can you call him late at night? Do his friends know about you? Can you show up at his job for lunch? Are you invited over for holidays? Are you around for his birthday? If you can answer "Yes" to the majority of these questions then you are headed in the right direction. Intimacy is important in every relationship. Look at the totality of your interactions so you can make a wise, grown-up decision based on the facts.

Disclaimer: We are not encouraging sex before marriage by any means, however it is a part of life. We recommend you incorporate these tips and follow your own morals and spiritual beliefs to arrive at your own decision.

MORE DUOver™ DATING TIPS:

- Don't give into the societal and media pressure to be actively dating someone, because if you do, you are likely to end up with someone who totally compromises what you need or want.

- Stick to your deal-breakers! Revisit your DUOver™ checklist often so when you are ready to date, your concerns will be well-defined in advance.

- When out on a date prepare three top things you want your date to know about you. This should be similar to your bucket list of things you want to accomplish and fun places you want to visit. Stay away from topics regarding your kids, past relationships, and work. It is a good idea to have a basic answer as to why you are single but keep it short. If you're divorced, end with, "It really was a learning experience and I wish him well." Be positive. Nothing heavy. The more you bash your ex and never accept responsibility for your contribution to the marriage the more the new person will infer there is a lot more to the story.

CHAPTER FIVE

DATING AFTER...

"If you decide to separate, be prepared for a divorce."

- The Matchmaking DUO™

COUNSELING ANYONE?

BEFORE you call it quits, try counseling. There will always be challenges in your marriage, but if you never fully address them or seek professional help to learn how to handle them, then you are giving up too easily. According to relationship expert Dr. John Gottman, less than 5% of divorcing couples seek marriage counseling. We want to get the word out that maintaining a marriage and dealing constructively with the difficulties that go along with it require relationship skills that we aren't always naturally born with. It's a good idea to seek help early when you feel constant stress and frustration in certain interactions with your spouse. If it's true that most marriages fail in seven years, it means that most people have been living unhappily for quite a while. There are certain skillsets that can be learned via marriage counseling that can help you save your marriage and foster long-term happiness.

In marriage counseling, you will learn:

- Effective communication skills; how to speak honestly without being angry.

- Processes to handle difficult issues you are currently facing and practice them both in sessions and at home.

- A greater understanding of who your spouse really is and what his needs are. Who knows? You may like him even more afterwards!

Again, counseling can help you get a better perspective on your marriage and provide the skills needed to overcome the challenges. A licensed counselor can work with you by evaluating your progress, mediating your conflict, and providing objective feedback. Keep in mind that there are thousands of marriage counselors and other relationship experts out there that you both can talk to, as well as going to your Pastor. We know that counseling does not work for everyone, but you should at least give it a try and remember to keep a positive attitude about your likelihood of success.

TAKE IT FROM ME

My husband and I tried counseling with a highly credentialed female marriage counselor that I chose. At the time, I knew that most of my marital issues were me being my independent, stubborn self. I went to this woman hoping that she would see my side and convince my husband to bail me out of the financial mess I had gotten us into. She totally did not understand my struggle. I was angry with her because she never told me what I wanted to hear. So I picked up the phone and called my girlfriends that think I am amazing at everything and supported my actions. Even when I was doing something that I had no business doing, they somehow found a way to tell me that it was OK. But deep down I knew I needed corrective behavior so I started to confide more in Kelli because she supported my marriage and would be my reality check and tell me the truth. I also became Kelli's go-to-person when she needed to hear the errors of her ways. When we are supporting each other we try to take our personal feelings out of the equation and advise the other to do what's right. It's like having an out of body experience. What I learned was that I had to own up to my contribution to the wreckage, accept responsibility, effectively listen and participate in a plan to correct my behavior.

SEPARATION

As a rule of thumb we try to keep couples from separating and recommend they work things out in the *same* room of the house. If you decide to separate, be prepared for divorce—even if you are living under the same roof. Working it out in the same room is the best advice we can offer because division only needs a small crack. Most people we have spoken to only separated to prove a point, "I bet when I leave he/she is going to come running back to me." Guess what, the other person took them seriously and left for good!

Many people muddy the waters even further by dating during separation. Like any new relationship, initially it can seem like the best thing in the world because your spouse is still on-deck but you're experimenting with something new. You think to yourself, *finally this person gets me!* However, over time the things that you initially had in common tend to wear off because chances are you have not changed and you were never supposed to be with this person in the first place.

"If you water your OWN grass every day, it will stay green."

-Granny Marie McIntosh

TAKE IT FROM ME

Studies show that it takes your mate 7-10 years to learn how to properly love you. The seven year itch was real for me. I was separated from my husband for two years. I moved to a different state to create distance. Entering the dating scene after being married for many years was more daunting than I cared to admit. I started to miss my husband and our great times together. All of a sudden it hit me like a ton of bricks that I still loved him and wanted him back. I spent many nights crying my eyes out to Kelli. Then one evening I had one of my special talks with my Granny Marie.

"Granny I miss my husband."

"Then you should go back and get him. You know, your stuff stinks too!"

"You're right Granny, I know."

I told her how I thought the grass was greener on the other side but realized how wrong I was. I will never forget the words she said to me that changed my relationship with my husband forever. She said, "Baby, if you water your *OWN* grass every day it will stay green." The next day I put forth my best effort to win my husband back and began watering my grass. It took months of initially talking and selling him on the new Tana. At first he didn't think I was serious. I explained to him that I had been working on myself through spiritual counseling and my innate relationship with God had become closer. That was 2011 and the old Tana never reared her Alpha head again and we have a stronger marriage than we both ever thought possible.

DIVORCE

"Never love someone so much that you lose yourself."

- The Matchmaking DUO™

Going through divorce whether amicable or not can be extremely painful. For those of you who opted for the traditional wedding vows, the officiator likely quoted, "for this reason a man shall leave his mother and father and the two shall become one flesh." (Eph. 5:31). It's painful because it's as if you're tearing away two souls to become one individual again. After a divorce you need to make time for yourself and rediscover who you are again as an individual. We recommend at least one year after your divorce is final before dating again. A sustainable new relationship is less likely to get on track or may take longer if you haven't had enough "me" time. You should also surround yourself with encouraging people to lift you up and push you in the right direction. If you are a spiritual person, stay connected to those people who remind you of who God says you are, not necessarily who you see in the mirror today.

We realize that sometimes you may want to just drop the ball and dismiss the hurt after divorce so you jump right into dating again. You take comfort in being attractive to another person and believe you are avoiding the rejection, the hurt, and other emotions that naturally came with the process. Before you know it, in the blink of an eye you are in another relationship confronted with the same issues you had previously, so your masking them didn't help.

Now, you are more scarred because you never dealt with, nor took the time to figure out what *you* could have done differently.

 **TAKE TWO**: During difficult times in your relationship be careful who you allow to be in your trusted inner circle. It's crucial to your well-being to have a true sister-friend. One bad apple can cause you to be negatively influenced by a third party and ruin your relationship with your husband. Women need other women to hold each other up. As business partners and great friends, we supported each other by praying and fasting together. While both of us were separated, we prayed for each other's marriages for nearly four months. Each time one of us wanted to give up the other stood in the gap and prayed harder. Even when we were angry at our spouses we convinced each other to hang in there. By the end of that year we were both back together with our husbands. As our marriages continued in peaks and valleys, Kelli and her husband decided to divorce.

TAKE IT FROM ME

Someone asked me after my divorce, "Kelli, what do you like to do?" I went blank. I was shocked because I had no idea. For the past nine plus years everything I did was based around my children and my husband. I could not believe how I had lost myself along the way in exchange for being a wife and mother. I didn't have an answer for the person but it was an eye-opening "Aha" moment and a perfect time for me to go back and reevaluate who Kelli was before she was married with children.

When I think about how I had evolved and who I wanted to be I get goosebumps. Being from New Jersey, I loved to try different restaurants and take a spontaneous drive to New York City with all of the excitement it brings from outdoor concerts to comedy shows. Or it was nothing for me and my girlfriends to travel to a tropical island and hit the jet ski or take a horseback riding excursion. I rediscovered my love for classical music and started listening to all of my favorites again from Rachmaninoff to Mozart. Turning it up in my car or at home was so soothing to my soul as my fingers fluttered on my virtual violin as I remembered every note I once played. It felt great to allow myself to go back to that wonderful place and time. The evolution of the new me was not something that happened overnight. There were many days of reflection and hurt which eventually opened up to a horizon that I could see up ahead. Ultimately it all led to forgiveness. Forgiveness of my ex and forgiveness of myself. I realized that replaying the "Why Me?" and that I was a "victim" over and over in my head was keeping me bound. I started to face myself in the mirror and asked myself questions like, *Were there signs in this marriage that I ignored?* I didn't wait to do things "traditionally" for it to end this way.

Once I started feeling like myself again, I was able to let go of the shame and feelings of defeat as an A+ personality—always wanting to win. I took time to grieve over my marriage. I searched deeper for God's voice and spiritual guidance. He showed me the greatness He placed within me again and I learned to live on purpose as opposed to who I saw in the mirror. I transferred my job from New York City to Charlotte to regain stability and spend more time with my three girls. I got involved in outside activities, got a bold haircut, dyed it foxy red, and went back to wearing heels for no reason at all. In my Sorority, I was known as "Glamour Gal" because I loved to enjoy life and look my best. I admit that I lost Kelli for a while somewhere along the way trying to be everything to everyone. But after having my "Come to Jesus" moment and taking a good, long look at myself in the mirror, my priority became to place myself at the top of the list where I found my happiness and confidence return. Being a better "you" makes a better "we." Take notice...Kelli's back!

DATING WITH CHILDREN

Many women are apprehensive about getting back into the dating scene with children. We have found that the primary reason is because they have been out of the dating regimen for so long and fear they are not up-to-date with the changing times. Women certainly realize that they look and feel different about relationships than they did years ago. As maturity sets in, they compare themselves to some of their younger friends with no children who never married. *"How can I possibly compete with her?,"* is a common thought that begins to set in. It can be a difficult transition being a mature single woman with kids after going through divorce.

It requires you to step out of your comfort zone and put forth effort and planning. If you have young kids, talk to your children about the possibility of dating. Let them know that you will be dating again and it may be a good idea to ask them what type of stepdad or stepmom would make them happy. Find out what qualities are important to them. Are they excited about the idea of you dating? Consider your child's personality to determine how to broach the subject.

Interview sitters a few months before you make the decision to start dating because it takes time to find ones you trust. It is important to feel very comfortable with them so you can have a good time and not worry about your kids. Have three main sitters on standby. When you are asked on a date, it doesn't look good that you have to cancel because you don't have childcare. Having a sitter lets the other person know that you are willing to make time for him. As things progress, don't let money be a deterrent that hinders you from going on a date. There are plenty of online deals and coupons that you can use to eventually take the kids with you and your date as things progress.

Don't introduce every person you date to your children. It is confusing and if it does not work out then your kids have to go through that same feeling of separation they did when their other parent left during the divorce. Once you and your significant other agree that the relationship is serious, you should involve the kids. If you don't engage them, then you are faced with the tensions of being with a great person for six months to a year that you have had time to bond with and your kids haven't.

Don't go crazy and try to have a date three or four nights a week and plan weekend trips. Keep a comfortable balance with your dating life and time with your children. The main point you want to get across with your children is that you have a new love interest, yet there will be always be time for you and them. You don't want them to resent the process and push back because they are not getting your time and attention like they once had.

MEET ASHLEY

Ashley had been married for ten years and she had two children from the marriage. Both she and her husband agreed to an amicable divorce and she has full physical custody of the kids. Her ex-husband has the children on alternating weekends. It's been nearly a year since the divorce was final and Ashley is ready to date again. She told us how her cousin divorced when her kids were similar ages to Ashley's kids. Her cousin's kids had total meltdowns when she wanted to go out and it got so bad that she stopped dating because no sitter wanted to keep them. Ashley did not want her kids to go through any more trauma from not having daddy at home.

Kelli: Ashley we understand how you feel. Tana and I have been through this before. We can tell you that the sooner you talk to the kids, get their buy-in, and set up a routine, the better off you all will be in the long run.

Ashley: Well that's great because I just can't imagine trying to enjoy myself on a date when I know my daughter is still bawling her eyes out at the front door.

Tana: So the most important thing we want to coach you for this session is the importance of having the conversation with your children that you will be dating again.

You can start by saying to the child, "I know that you understand mommy and daddy are not together anymore but just know that we love you very much. Since daddy and I are divorced, mommy is ready to have adult time and go out more. What type of person do you think would be good for mommy to date? What type of person do you think would be good for you?"

ASHLEY'S DUOVER™

For divorced women it is important to begin separating what worked in your marriage and what didn't.

Step 1: The Marriage Mirror - Consider what you liked about your ex and if those are the same characteristics you are looking for in a new relationship. What would you change? What are the things you learned about being a wife that you would do differently? What would your ex say about you?

Step 2: Talking to Children: Make this serious conversation into a fun one. Allow the kids to have input. Make it appear to be a game by asking them questions about the type of person that would be perfect for mommy. Let them know you will be interviewing babysitters to see who they are comfortable with. Reiterate that you need adult time at least once a week to go out and have fun like they do with their friends. Reassure them that there will be a night just for mommy and them as well. Make sure you spend quality time with them during the week with no television, emails, or cell phone distractions. Also, set bedtime boundaries and stick to them. If bedtime is 9PM then make sure you have addressed all of their nighttime needs like a drink of water, a tummy ache, school work, or any other "emergency" so that you can have uninterrupted time on the phone getting to know the new man in your life.

Men today are looking for more feedback. For example, on the first date don't be afraid to say, "I'm having a great time." Keep the lines of communication open. Don't just sit by the phone waiting for his call. If he's on your mind, give him a call not worrying about who called last or appearing too forward. This way, he doesn't have to wonder how you felt about him or the date in general. As long as you are responsive, he knows that things are starting out positive. Put aside any old-fashioned models in your head that as a woman you are supposed to wait for him to contact and court you while you sit idly by. In many cases that would be nice, but realistically don't be surprised if it does not happen. What we've learned over the years is that the assertive woman get's the catch. So, if there was a spark, great conversation and lots of laughs, you'd better quickly let him know that or someone else will beat you to it!

CHAPTER SIX

YOUR LOVE LANGUAGE DUOVER™

*Love is patient and kind. Love is not jealous or boastful or
proud or rude.
Love does not demand its own way.
Love is not irritable, and it keeps no record of when it has
been wronged...
Love never gives up, never loses faith, is always hopeful, and
endures through every circumstance.
Love will last forever...*

- 1 Cor. 13:4-8

FEELING loved is different for each person. One person may need
lots of hugs while another may need to take action—doing kind
things to let someone know you care. We both are avid fans of Gary
Chapman's five love languages: 1) Words of Affirmation; 2) Acts
of Service; 3) Receiving of Gifts; 4) Quality Time and 5) Physical
Touch. All of these languages can be easily understood, yet can be
incoherent if you are not targeting your significant other's specific
love language needs. We can't stress enough the importance of identifying your mate's love language and keeping the "love tank" full.
Make sure you are clearly aware of what makes him tick. So if it's
words of affirmation or quality time, become an expert at it. Don't
be fooled into thinking that you can love him the way you want to
be loved. His love language may be different from yours. It's definitely well worth your time to take Chapman's 30-question assessment. Once you identify your partner's love language you should
focus on ensuring that your actions are in tune with what he desires.

TAKE TWO: For years we traveled for work and spent hours (sometimes two days) in the kitchen making lavish meals for our families before our departure. We both thought we were saving our husbands' time and they could just heat the food in the oven or microwave and feed the kids. To our surprise, years later, we discovered that neither of our husbands cared what we cooked. They would rather have ordered pizza or eat turkey and cheese sandwiches with us at home cuddled up watching a movie or an adult night on the town before we hit the road. Instead, we were both in our homes preparing meals for the entire week and exhausted! We later realized that we were speaking two different love languages. We recommend that couples get together and learn each other's love language early on to eliminate time spent engaging in activities that are not pleasing to the other person. It is bound to save your relationship a lot of tension and confusion.

Words of Affirmation

If your significant other's love language is Words of Affirmation, make sure that your words are heartfelt and used often. When he takes on a challenging task at work or helps the kids with their homework, let him know how much you appreciate his efforts in doing whatever it takes to help his family. For this person, *action does not speak louder than words,* and all of your acts of love may go unnoticed. Train your vocabulary to use encouraging, kind, and humble words and you will see a drastic change in his response to you.

Wife: Honey you did an excellent job on that new project. When I saw your proposal, it made me light up inside. I know you'll get the promotion!

Husband: Thanks sweetheart, that means a lot to me.

Wife: Thank you for mowing the lawn. I love the way you take care of our home, not to mention watching you work up a sweat from the window, turns me on.

Husband: Thanks babe, I love making you happy.

Acts of Service

"Learn to speak your partner's language of love. It's scientifically proven that men who do housework get more sex."

- Dr. Laura Berman

The "Doer" in your life is likely to choose "Acts of Service" as his primary love language. "Doing" is a direct extension of a person. It is as if his hand is physically on everything that is connected to you to express his love. Therefore, all of his extremely helpful acts like cleaning the house, putting gas in your car, or handling a personal situation on your behalf are all genuine acts of service to demonstrate his love and affection for you. Be sure to thank him for making your life easier. In addition, if Acts of Service is your primary love language, let your spouse know as soon as possible how much satisfaction you get in cooking his favorite meal or handling household paperwork that gets on his nerves.

Receiving of Gifts

Gifts are a visual expression of love. At the heart of scripture, an expression of love is giving (John 15:13). If your significant other's love language is the Receiving of Gifts please know that money is not the focus of this language. Instead, it is the fact that you thought enough about your spouse to stop off and buy a gift in the first place. There is something about your mate holding a tangible item in his hands that serves a reminder of your love for him. It may be a good idea to search and purchase gifts in advance so that you will always have something readily available for a special occasion or "just because" I love you. For example, if he is a sports fan make your list of the customized memorabilia of his favorite team.

Quality Time

This was a big factor in both of our marriages. Our husbands could care less about dinner and more about being cuddled on the sofa. Neither of us realized back then that "time" was a strong love communicator. Even with all of the distractions today and many of you working hectic schedules and raising kids, giving your spouse uninterrupted, dedicated time focused solely on him will work wonders for your relationship. If his love language is Quality Time, going for walks, watching sunsets together, or doing nothing but staring into each other's eyes will make him happy. Quality time leads to more honest, open communication, and should feel like a "date night," sometimes without even leaving the house. Just like you have a Wish List for future online purchases, talk with your spouse about things he'd like to do in the near future and make a Quality Time Wish List of those activities. Do everything in your power to check an activity off the Wish List every few weeks.

Physical Touch

Chances are, whenever someone mentions "Physical Touch," people immediately think of sex. Touch is so much more than that, and there are probably people out there who will agree that it can be better than sex. It's holding hands, hugging, kissing, and caressing.

If you didn't come from a "touchy-feely" family then this is something that you will have to make a conscious effort of doing often. Therefore, make sure you engage in a physical connection with this type of guy at least twice a day. If that means a kiss in the morning and a kiss at night, then do it. Hold hands. Stroke his back while he is reading the paper or working on the computer...and yes, always be a ready, willing and able sex partner!

Remember, it is rare for spouses to have identical love languages. Make a commitment to genuinely hone in on your spouse's love language and you will see how it becomes a great communication tool to strengthen your relationship.

CHAPTER SEVEN

YOUR ALPHA FEMALE DUOVER™

The shoes on my feet
I've bought it
The clothes I'm wearing
I've bought it
The rock I'm rockin'
'Cause I depend on me...

- Independent Woman - Destiny's Child

IT'S no secret. By the time women achieve their educational and career goals they are likely in their late thirties or early forties. Their biological clocks are ticking a lot slower and colleagues and family are telling inside jokes behind their backs about not having kids yet. *Where has all the time gone?* They wonder. *Can I still have the husband and two children I envisioned before college?* Unfortunately, this is a dilemma that Alpha women constantly face. Men in executive level positions are usually married with children and have far less worries about their child's day-to-day activities, or traveling overnight or internationally for business. Instead, they are free to focus on attaining promotions, tenure and other levels of advancement. Let's face it, as women, we are not the same after having kids. The universe looks and feels different. Children really change perspectives.

We all have heard stories of successful women whether corporate professionals or celebrities, who reached the pinnacle of their careers who believe that they may have missed the window for true love, happiness and children. As Alpha women, your intelligence, self-confidence and ambition may intimidate men. If you act like you don't need a man for anything, why should he hang around? Men need to feel useful and appreciated more often than not. It's never too late for love and if you're an Alpha female you're in a great position to find it by making a few tweaks.

MEET SHARON

We spoke to Sharon on the phone three times before she decided to invest in her future happiness. Sharon is an accomplished professional with two advanced degrees in science from MIT. She is currently a high level executive with a Fortune 100 company, no children, and never found time for a relationship. Climbing the corporate ladder consumed her, and she fears finding love may be too late. Sharon has already admitted to us that traditional, subservient roles of women in marriage would be a major challenge for her. She manages several hundred people, including a ton of men, and the thought of listening or even submitting to her husband is a sign of weakness that is foreign to her. She's been a leader and the boss for over 20 years. Sharon told us that it's going to be hard to turn it on and off., not to mention the frightening thoughts of becoming a sexy vixen after 5 o'clock to make a man happy. She has apprehensive thoughts as to *how she can possibly conform or compete with other women who are ready and willing?* She arrived promptly at our offices in her St. John Collection navy and cream tweed skirt, navy turtleneck, and white freshwater pearls. The only sign of makeup were two strokes of mascara on each eye. Her hair wasn't pulled back in a bun, but it was blown straight with each side behind her ears.

> **Sharon:** Nice to finally meet you in person. *She motioned for us to sit down. She pulled out a leather Burberry portfolio and opened it to a blank legal-sized page, while grabbing her sterling and leather Aspinal of London pen, which certainly caught our eye.* I'm still a bit hesitant about this whole process but I know it's pretty much now or never. I

am interested in finding some type of companionship. If marriage happens then great, but I really feel it's time to get out there and at least meet eligible men, which is something *very* new to me.

Kelli: Well we're glad you've taken this step because it requires a serious commitment on your part to really dig deep and focus on your strengths, weaknesses, relationship goals and what you desire in an ideal mate.

Tana: I know you're no stranger to hard work and dedication as we have thoroughly reviewed the online profile questionnaire you submitted.

Kelli: OK so let's talk about the elevator pitch we mentioned to you on the phone. What do you have so far?

Sharon: Like I've said, this is very new to me. I guess I want him to know where I work, where I went to school, and…

Tana: Sharon, I don't mean to cut you off. Your job and education are certainly important but men don't need to know that in the first fifteen seconds. A man can tell a little bit about your background just by the way you carry yourself, your style, and your tone. What do you like to do for fun? Do you have any hobbies? These are topics we want you to prepare to share in your initial conversations on a date as opposed to your three-page resume.

Sharon: I love to travel and take off two weeks twice a year and go abroad to exotic locations. Last year I went to Spain and Switzerland and this year I'm going to Australia and Bora Bora.

Kelli: Traveling is a great ice-breaker. Let's think of some stories from your adventures while on vacation. We want your date to see your fun side and connect with you as a person, rather than a professional. One way to get a man's attention is to look him in the eye, and then flash a warm smile. It let's him know you're approachable for conversation.

SHARON'S DUOVER™

For women like Sharon we start off with coaching exercises to soften their image. She looked and talked like the boss. Often times when she spoke it was as if she were directing us to work on a project. She had a strong personality but we saw her eagerness to make changes.

Here are a few of our recommendations to Sharon:

Step 1: Image consulting - We suggested that she alter her wardrobe with more color. The navy and pearls were OK for work but she needed a transitional look for after work. To help her look more approachable, we recommended changing her style of dress to still look powerful, but not be afraid to wear a colorful blouse under a tailored suit. Adding a new haircut and glossy lip color were bound to get her noticed.

Step 2: Soften Approach - The first thing we did was develop coaching exercises to help her soften her approach. When she stepped into the room we felt like we were about to have our year-end performance evaluations. Sharon had to realize that everyone she meets in life is not a member of her staff. We advised her that it was OK for her to use more terms of endearment in her vocabulary like "hon," "babe," or "dear," to appear more human. She needed to also work on developing her personal life with interests and hobbies to give her a comfortable work/life balance.

TAKE IT FROM ME

Growing up in a primarily single parent home, my mom did everything she could to give me a good life. I didn't have many examples of healthy relationships. I desired a sound marriage and a real true-love for a long-lasting relationship. However, when times got rough, the women in my family were strong, independent and not afraid to bail if need be. They often declared, "I've had enough and I can do bad by myself. I'm going to raise these children on my own and make ends meet by any means necessary!" Even though I wanted something different for myself, I fell into the same cyclical pattern that my family did. It was to the point that my strong, domineering, independent female characteristics landed me in a two-year separation from my husband as well.

In 2003, after a successful business trip I decided to treat myself to a new car without even mentioning it to my husband. A colleague and I were leaving the airport and I asked her to drive me straight to the Toyota dealership. My husband declared that I didn't need a new car previously, but I told him I had just received a promotion and I deserved it. I later drove home with a new, Black 2003 Toyota Camry fresh off the showroom floor. I thought I could do whatever I wanted, whenever I wanted. After all, it was my money! I was an independent woman. The car was nothing compared to my next purchase.

When I married my husband I moved into his three-bedroom home. We merged our blended family. The dynamics were his two children from his previous marriage, and he was raising his ex-wife's daughter from her former relationship as his own. I entered the relationship with two children; one from a previous marriage and the other from a previous relationship. There were seven people living in a tiny house. I thought I was going to go bonkers. Every time I complained about needing a bigger house my husband would remind me that the kids would be off to college soon. He insisted that we could not afford a bigger house at that time. What did he know? He was only a financial advisor!

In 2005, I discounted everything he said and took my oldest son with me to begin the construction of my 4,300 square foot home which had 5 bedrooms, 4 bathrooms, a basement, and a perfect office for me. Finally, plenty of space for all! I had a six-figure income so I didn't need my husband's money for the down payment, nor his credit. I swore my son to secrecy and we visited the home and took pictures of the building phase of the house often. Three weeks before the house was completed and I was preparing to move in, I told my husband, "I built a house." I'm moving and if you want to come you are welcome. I'm moving with or without you. I can't take this small house any longer!"

Early in my marriage, that was my attitude—take or leave it. I knew deep inside it wasn't OK but it was the pattern that I had seen growing up and it became the pattern I intended to follow. Against his better judgment, my husband reluctantly moved with me. My plan blew up in my face. Shortly after the move I was laid off and we were house poor. Why didn't I listen to my husband?

ALPHA FEMALE DUOver™ TIP:

Tana's Lessons Learned:

- I learned that I needed to turn off being an executive and transition into being a wife and mother after 5 PM. In hindsight, I didn't allow my husband to protect and provide for us. He was very capable, but I did not give him the opportunity to be the man he was called to be. He had all the tools and that's what attracted me to him in the very beginning. He was a West Point Military Academy graduate, a natural leader. I realized that I was being controlling. If I allowed him to step into the role he was designed for, things may have been different. Men are natural fixers and want to feel needed. I thought that by me allowing him to be the man, I in turn would appear weak and lose my freedom.

- Don't be afraid to ask for help and let him know how much you appreciate what he's done. It's very easy to make yourself believe you don't need a man when you're successful. But loneliness is universal so make a list of all of the ways he fulfills your needs and make sure you celebrate them with him and share with others all of the great qualities he adds to your life.

- It is OK to be humble and admit where you are wrong. It was my "Aha" moment. I apologized and took responsibility for my actions.

- Stay in your lane and identify your role as a wife and mother and adhere to that role. Don't make decisions on impulse just because you can. Compromise and take your time until you both reach an agreeable decision. Learn to understand the reason behind his decision-making. So now, when I want to make a purchase we have an established budget that we've agreed upon where I don't need permission. Anything over the budget requires discussion.

- Most important, if you are making him feel less than a man, someone else will!

CHAPTER EIGHT

YOUR DNA DUOVER™

"Pedigree doesn't trump DNA."

- Niche Faulkner

THE Tibetan Mastiff from China is reported to be the most expensive dog in the world selling for over $2 million. However, if it's inbred, it's worthless. In other words, it can be beautiful on the outside but a mess on the inside. Did you ever consider the DNA of the person you are connected with? Most women don't. We get so distracted by looks, income, status, and material possessions that conversations about his blood-line never surface. You need to know family history and traits. If you don't, it's just like putting apples, oranges, and peanuts into your blender and expecting it to taste like a delicious strawberry banana smoothie. Knowing the DNA of the person you are with will help you make an informed decision about taking the relationship to another level. Without this knowledge, once the relationship progresses and children are involved you realize, *Lord help me, these kids are crazy!*

DNA is a genetic cell that is capable of replication. It determines an individual's hereditary characteristics. In fact, it's just like breeding animals where their legacy or bloodline is very important. How often has your parent said to you, "You're just like your mother or you're just like your father." Sometimes it's a compliment; most times it's not. When parents make these statements their misguided because the children are part of their DNA as well, but not by choice. Your kids' habits, both good and bad, are the spitting image of the two of you. It's not until you're facing challenges with your children down the line that you realize they are replicating negative characteristics that are coming back to bite you. You get frustrated as you struggle to correct behavior that isn't in line with your values.

It's important that we speak to young women and tell them to be careful who they lay down with because they really need to know his DNA. Even as Christians, we know we can break generational curses, but you need to know exactly what you are getting sooner than later. At the end of the day you should go back to your DUOver™ deal-breaker list and consider whether his DNA traits are something you can or cannot live with. Pay attention to those characteristics in his family as you will likely have to deal with these traits for two or three generations.

MEET DAWN

No one really thinks about DNA when they are about to enter into a committed relationship. When women sit around with their girlfriends and if the subject of DNA does come up, the conversation may sound like this, "All I know is that he's fine, his daddy's fine, and his brothers are even finer!" After the laughs wear off and you are a year and a half into the relationship, you realize that complete "fine-ness" comes with a high price. He cheats on you, his daddy cheats on his mom, and his brothers have never been married, not to mention the lightbulb that just came on when you realize his brothers have introduced you to numerous female "friends" during that time. Can a man's womanizer DNA change? In most cases NO, unless they've made a conscious effort or have a strong desire of their own to change!

In walks Dawn. We do a double take because she is the spitting image of Tracee Ellis Ross; even down to her style of fashion. Dawn has studied abroad at Oxford and has an advanced degree from Dart-mouth. She has been in several on-again, off-again relationships, and can't seem to find her match. Rodney, the last guy she was involved with, broke her number one rule: Never go out with a guy who looks better than me! She learned from experience that guys that fine bring nothing but drama because they are every woman's dream. But Rodney felt different. He was the most intelligent and charismatic man she had ever met. A total package. An extremely successful Alpha Male to whom she was instantly attracted to. Of course Rodney knew he was fine but downplayed it every chance he got. He acknowledged that his brothers and father were ladies' men, but that was *never* who he was. She fell for him because he was a man of his word—at least in the beginning. He was so attentive to her every need and treated her like a true queen. Dawn was sure the ring was coming, to the point where she started making her own plans.

Out of the blue, Rodney began to change. His charisma and demeanor were quickly fading. He would be excited one minute and then totally angry and depressed the next. He started pulling disappearing acts four or five days at a time and would be angry when Dawn confronted him about his whereabouts. Then, all of sudden the old, totally wonderful Rodney would appear. Dawn was confused, but relatively happy. She had a close relationship with his mother so she decided to talk to her about Rodney's mood swings.

> *DAWN:* So I invited Rodney's mom to lunch at the Cheesecake Factory because it's her favorite place. His mom and I hit it off from the very beginning so I felt comfortable bringing this to her. I told her how Rodney had been experiencing mood swings lately and then disappearing for days on end. She seemed very worried and patted my hand across the table while nodding in agreement as I was speaking.

> *TANA:* Maybe she was expecting you to come to her sooner or later.

> *DAWN:* Yes that's exactly what it seemed like. She told me how much she really liked me and hoped that Rodney and

I married, but she wanted me to know a few things about him. She swore me to secrecy. Basically she told me that both Rodney and his father are bipolar and they are on medication. She said that Rodney had been under a lot of pressure with work and became involved with some other women. He recently stopped taking his medication regularly. She assured me that Rodney intends to marry me and wants to come clean about all of this.

KELLI: So how did you respond?

DAWN: I got out of my seat and scooted next to her in her booth and gave her the biggest hug. We both let a few tears fall, wiped our faces and continued with lunch without mentioning it again. I was dying to confront Rodney, but I made a promise and I knew that his situation would rear its head again anyway. Sure enough, two weeks later it happened.

TANA: What happened?

DAWN: Rodney whisked me away for a weekend to the Caribbean and said he had a surprise for me. It was the most romantic weekend I had ever experienced. On our last night he had our chef make all of my favorite seafood dishes. Immediately after dinner he got down on one knee and pulled out a five-karat pear-shaped ring. I felt light-headed. My emotions were in overdrive. I kept thinking, *When is he going to tell me about the other woman and his bipolar disorder?* Instead, I hugged him and said "Yes." Once he put the ring on he said, Dawn, there is something I have to tell you. My heart stopped. He told Dawn about his bipolar disorder but assured her it was under control.

Dawn held on to the ring for a few days weighing what Rodney had told her. She decided that she could live with his bipolar disorder because millions of people are diagnosed with this illness and function well on medication. For the entire year and a half when Rodney was taking his medication he was truly prince charming. However, the thing that she could not live with was his cheating which he always resorted to when he stopped taking his medication. Rodney told Dawn that he was briefly involved with *two* other women that his brothers introduced him to. He assured her that neither of them meant anything to him and that she was the love of his life. He even had his mother call her to reiterate his plea. Dawn broke it off and gave Rodney his ring back. She knows her true love is out there and has trusted us to help her find him.

DAWN'S DUOVER™

Dawn indicated that she and Rodney's mother hit it off early. Of course that's a great thing, however if you don't talk about substantive family issues, over time they will come back to haunt you. It's unfortunate how society praises little boys for being a "heartbreaker." Does it annoy you when an adult says to an adorable male toddler, "how many girlfriends do you have?" The fact that we think it is OK to engrain this type of behavior into our male children is wrong. We should all strive to train up our children the right way.

> ***Step 1:*** <u>Family Relationships</u> - Keep a watchful eye when you are invited to family events and around his immediate family. Is his family close? Are they trustworthy? Have you seen them let each other down? If so, there is a possibility your guy will do the same thing. Are many family members married? Dawn saw first-hand that it was OK with Rodney's family that his two brothers have several women. Dawn never

realized that womanizing and not being faithful is a genetic thing and she did not want that for her future child. Finally, Dawn recognized that Rodney's father was his role model and that Rodney and his brothers were just emulating what they saw their entire lives.

DNA DUOver™ TIPS:

- If you want your children to be college educated but hook up with someone who views college as unimportant to him or his family, then you cannot get angry when your child has no desire to go to college.

- Have a serious talk with your significant other and his family. Are there major psychological issues in the family? What are their beliefs? Do they support marriage? Are there successful marriages in the family? For those that are married, is it OK for the husbands to step out with other women?

CHAPTER NINE

YOUR HAPPILY EVER AFTER DUOVER™

"Happily married couples aren't smarter or richer or more psychologically astute than others. The more emotionally intelligent a couple, the better able they are to understand, honor and respect each other and their marriage."

- John Gottman & Nan Silver

I F only our elders told us the real deal about marriage. As little girls growing up we all believed Disney's fairy tale that our prince charming is going to choose us over all the other girls and we're going to live happily ever after—forever. Now it's your big day and as you walk down the aisle everyone wears big smiles and offers congratulations. You're on cloud nine thinking everything after this moment will be blissful and peachy, which is the furthest from the truth. In hindsight, did you ever wonder how many of your guests were actually laughing behind your back? All of the married ones know that the daily work begins immediately after the wedding is over. If you don't put an effort into your marriage each and every day it will not be enjoyable. Like our parents, most of us didn't know what to expect. They never talked about what happens in-between time and what to prepare for. We asked married couples why this was the case and the consensus was that either they were hoping that the new couple's outcome would be different from theirs or they did not want to ruin the moment. Historically, no one told them, so they just decided not to say anything. Who knows? Maybe since they had to figure it out for themselves they expected us to do the same.

Did you grow up in a secret family? You know, where everything was hush-hush, and no one ever talked about sex, or arguments and strife were glazed over the surface to look like everything was fine. If so, chances are you were in for a real shock when the prince charming phase faded and you didn't know how to respond.

When you talked to family and friends you realize that you and your spouse are not the only ones going through a rough patch. Everybody does. Why didn't anyone tell you sooner? What could you have done differently? Why doesn't anyone want to tell young people the down and dirty, ins and outs about marriage?

> *"By all means marry. If you get a good wife, you'll become happy, if you get a bad one, you'll become a philosopher."*
>
> **- Socrates**

Despite the grim statistics of divorce and the media portrayal of dysfunctional relationships, more than two million people get married each year. Falling in love is inevitable. Did you know our brains produce elevated levels of a chemical called dopamine which controls our attention and focus? This chemical triggers those fleeting thoughts, *He's my one and only forever!* Your head-over-heels experience causes you to spend the entire day thinking solely of that other person and you're longing to be with him or her. Therefore, no matter what anyone says, when it feels *this* good, you're going to take that walk down the aisle, radiating like the sun. Besides, the bridal stores and catering halls are counting on you!

TAKE IT FROM ME

One of the mistakes I made during my marriage is that I put our children first. Growing up as the youngest child, I really had no experience with being the "mom" and all that it entailed. In hindsight, it appeared these things came naturally to women who have huge families or younger siblings around, so caring for children is like second nature for some. But here I was, newly married, new baby, and I was determined to conquer this new role as a mom and forgot about being a wife. With only 24-hours in a day, the majority of my time was spent adjusting to changing diapers, feedings, keeping the house together, and I thought I was "doing something." Little did I know, I had skipped over the "wife" class. The "Aha" moment for me was when I learned a husband needs to feel valued in the family circle and although there's a new member or two or three, your unit as a couple should remain front and center. With that framework, everything else can fall into place.

"The phrase "Don't ask don't tell" apparently is not just for the military."

- The Matchmaking DUO™

Isn't it ironic that although many of our grandparents had 10 or more children, sex was never discussed and you knew you were expected to be a "good girl" and not labeled as "fast" or "loose." But they never told us when or how to turn it on and what things they did in the bedroom, which apparently happened quite often, to keep each other happy for years on end.

Older generations never talked about deep family dysfunctions nor how to resolve conflicts. How many times did our parents or grandparents hide a family secret of infidelity or a teen "sent away" to hide a pregnancy. But what's so secretive about getting married? They should be shouting to the mountaintops everything they learned in the 40 plus years of marriage and passing that wisdom down. Things like sex should no longer be considered "nasty." Maybe our parents and grandparents didn't let us in on this because they were unaware that is was something we needed or worth sharing. It was all learned behavior because they spent most of their life learning through trial and error too. This practice has been prevalent for years throughout history within relationships, i.e. infidelity, children outside of the marriage, molestation within families, etc. But it's time to revamp this behavior for ourselves and generations to come. Hopefully this will change and our knowledge and experience can be shared with the younger generation to help them. It starts with us.

TAKE IT FROM ME

When I think about the generational differences I recall all of my family in the hospital room surrounding my grandmother as she was near death. While gasping for air we noticed she was trying to say something. We leaned in closer and to our surprise she mustered the strength in an audible whisper to say, "Do not embarrass me." The difference in mindset of former generations was that preserving the family name was more important than sharing stories of challenges and mistakes. Although she and my grandfather taught me so many overall life lessons through all that they accomplished, there are many questions left unanswered as to how they made it through 50+ years of marriage…

MEET CARLA

We're not surprised when we meet clients who say their parents still treat them like 10-year-olds! We hear stories of parents who try to control every aspect of their adult daughter's life, such as what they should do for a living, how they should spend their money, and who they should go out with. Controlling parents can cause long-term emotional damage to their children and often it's because of their own insecurities or personal agenda.

Carla is the oldest of three children. Her father was a city sanitation worker and her mother worked in the cafeteria of the local hospital. Carla's parents wanted so much more for her and saved every penny they had for her to be the first one in the family to go to college. Wanting more than anything to please her parents, Carla allowed them to choose the college she would attend, her major, and ultimately her friends—no guy was ever good enough. Early on, she thought it was a good thing that her parents did everything for her. She didn't have to worry about what to eat, what to wear, or how she should spend her time.

Now at 46, childless, and dateless, she cannot believe how she allowed her parents to control her life without ever questioning or having input. She majored in business and spent over 20 years working in product development and strategic marketing when all along she wanted to be a lawyer. She told us how when she was a child she watched old *Perry Mason* shows with her parents and reenacted cases for her younger siblings. Her mother encouraged her to pursue law, but by the time she reached high school, her father told her that women can't be really good lawyers and that she should focus on business. Always "pleasing" Carla obliged because deep down inside she felt guilty of their sacrifice for her.

Carla: I have all of the makings of success. Impressive title, beautiful home, designer clothing, a weekly standing salon appointment, and I drive a Range Rover. My parents are well taken care of, and so is the rest of my family. But am I happy? Do I have a family of my own? No! Sometimes I look at my parents and I hate them for never allowing me to utter a word against them. My opinion did not count so I stopped offering. I just went along with *their* program. So after all my hard work and dedication to my parents, I ended up being the breadwinner for four grown people. You know, I'm still mad at them sometimes!

CARLA'S DUOVER™

Carla still gets annoyed with herself because she feels like a little girl around her parents. We knew this was something that she wanted to repair because she feared it would spill over into her new relationship. She wasn't ready for the confrontation, but decided to write a letter to them instead expressing her guilt and hurt for how her life ended up thus far.

Step 1: <u>Write a letter</u> - Even if your parents never read it, the letter serves as a therapeutic event to rid you of your hate, guilt, fears or other insecurities in being raised by controlling parents. The letter serves as a way to get the issue off your chest and bring closure to the past. For those clients that have read the letter to their parents they are sometimes surprised when their parents response is that they had no idea that their child felt that way. In other instances, some parents continue to be in denial, but our clients are better prepared, knowing that this exercise is not for their parents, but instead, for their own healing. They can now be at peace with this issue regardless of the outcome.

IN SICKNESS & IN HEALTH

Often times we overlook the part of the marital vows "in sickness and in health". This is such an important part of your vows so be sure to choose someone who will take this to heart. We all need to know that someone has our back and will love and support us when unforeseen circumstances arise like one spouse develops cancer or other serious illness. Statistics show that patient-divorce breakdowns by sex indicated that when a man became ill, only 3% of those men's marriages ended in divorce. However, when the woman became ill, the number rose to 21%. One point to note is that the studies did not look at what types of marriages the couples had before the illness. Doctors have concluded that when women are faced with life and death challenges they hunker down and take care of family. Some men on the other hand, don't know how to handle the pressure of taking care of their wife and other daily responsibilities so they just leave.

 **TAKE TWO:** So many women have shared their stories of heartbreak after being diagnosed with breast cancer and their husbands walking out on them. These women thought they were in strong marriages only to find that their husbands could not handle them being ill or transformed in any way. Put yourself in their shoes for a moment. Before getting married, we ask you to visualize a catastrophe and ask yourself, would this person be there for me? Would he bathe, clothe, and feed me if necessary? It's difficult to imagine this we know, but it's important to feel confident that they would. What if they couldn't perform sexually like they

used to? Is that now a deal-breaker? We discussed in earlier chapters that other qualities are more important than good looks and great sex because if those two things go away unexpectedly, you're up a creek without a paddle. Choose wisely.

READINESS QUOTIENT

Loving you gave me something new
That I've never felt
Never dreamed of
Something's changed
No it's not the feeling I had before
Oh it's much much more...

- Love Ballad, **LTD**

When you are dating someone how do you know if you are ready for commitment? Everything that we have discussed thus far involves taking an honest and thorough evaluation of yourself. If you are ready to make the plunge into a committed relationship consider this quiz to be your self-check. Be sure to keep track of how many topics below definitely apply to you, then check out the results at the end. You should be proud of yourself if you pass because many of these factors overlap on your DUOver™ deal-breaker list anyway.

1) **You're Ready To Share Your Time and Space**

So you've been single for quite a while now and have enjoyed going and coming as you please. But, now it is more important to be considerate of not only your time but also reallocating your schedule to make room for him too. Have you made a little space for his love in your life?

2) You Consider His "Likes" and "Dislikes" Too

Do you know his favorite juice or snacks? What would make him smile? Do you think he's thinking about you like you're thinking about him?

3) His Words Mirror His Actions

Does everything he says match what he does? Do you have full access to him any time of the day or night? That's a great sign. Plus, it shows you're able to see his worth and his value as a potential partner.

4) You're Comfortable Being Vulnerable and Transparent

Have you opened up to him beyond your comfort level? Oftentimes relationships function on the surface. But it's really important to peel back and share additional layers of your heart. As a result, you will develop a deeper level of intimacy and it will help him piece together the puzzle of how you arrived to be the woman you are today.

5) You Can Trust Him To Make Decisions On Your Behalf And Vice Versa

It's important to observe his decision-making patterns and share yours as well. Be prepared to compromise and trust him to step in on your behalf when needed.

6) You're Considering Both Your Goals and Your Futures

Yes, you have goals and dreams. But, guess what? He does, too. Have you considered how to incorporate both? Make his goals equally as important and embrace them as if they are yours.

7) You Know His Family and Friends, And They Know You Too

If you show up at his job for lunch, will his coworkers know your name? Are you invited to family gatherings, holiday dinners? Do his close friends know and embrace you as part of the crew? That's a great sign that he is proud of you and is thinking long-term.

8) You've Discussed the 'Future' Together

Are topics such as the desire to have children, merging families and finances as well as faith expectations openly discussed? Can you clearly see how things would work out? Another amazing sign you can move forward.

How Many Did You Answer Favorably?

1-4? - Give it more time! No need to rush things and get serious before you're ready.

5-7? - You're getting somewhere. Discuss "what's next" together and make sure your relationships goals are a match.

ALL 8? - Congratulations, you've arrived!

DUOver™ Workshop
BELIEVING IN LOVE AGAIN

By this time in our lives, we've all had our feelings or heartbroken at least once. The pain is excruciating. There isn't a prescription or over-the-counter medicine that will take it away. The only cure is time! Will love happen for you again? We say ABSOLUTLEY! But you have to believe it. We discuss in our workshop how important it is to ensure positivity. Whatever you put out there, you will get back in return. We continuously tell our clients that we believe it for them until they are able to believe it for themselves.

3 Take-aways:

1) Write down why you are worthy of love and your positive attributes.

2) Post it everywhere imaginable; i.e. the refrigerator, mirror, office, your car.

3) Memorize it and repeat it daily!

DUOver™ Workshop
HOW TO GET THE RING

Ladies, we found out that we have been doing it wrong all along. During our interviews and conversations with men of different cultures, ethnicities, and those currently living across the globe, the consensus is the same: Support, Great Sex and Direct Communication. In this workshop we spill the beans on the ring-secrets with examples, role play, and how to get the results you want... THE DIAMOND!

BLENDED FAMILIES

"Your children will see what you're all about by what you live rather than what you say."

- Dr. Wayne Dyer

Chances are if you are in your second marriage either or both of you have children. It is important to identify each child in the relationship and have an individual connection to each one. Open communication is key. Preferably have conversations with your kids and your new children when you are considering marrying. All of the kids need to spend time together to see how they get along. Your individual parent-child relationships should be one-on-one time and not just as a group because every child's needs are different. For example, we recommend that you have an occasional date night individually with each child and learn their personalities. This also gives the child something to look forward to and demonstrates your commitment to him or her.

It is also important for you to connect with the exes because it is for the greater good of the children. All of the adults must have a united front to raise the children together because this will help them become stronger, wiser, well-balanced, and more diverse than they otherwise would be. When your children see that you don't hate their mom or dad they will have much more respect for you and not trump one over the other. Another key point is to include the other parent in decision-making and in the child's day-to-day activities. The children should know that they can ask their mom or dad their opinion on a matter. Always seek inclusion. Just remember the kids are the glue that holds a blended family together.

One child may be struggling more than the other but you need to take notice regardless if the other children are fine. Both parents should have a conversation with each other and agree on the disciplinary action for the child and include the biological parent and step-parent. This way there won't be a disciplining conflict. You should all agree collectively so you are on the same page. This type of give-and-take with the exes will take work, but it can happen over time.

TAKE IT FROM ME

My mother is still good friends with my stepmother because when my father picked me up for visits, he and my stepfather would have a drink while my mother and stepmother chatted the entire time. I clearly remember standing in the corner with my arms folded ready to go and begin my weekend with my dad.

Similarly, my husband and I are great friends with his ex-wife and we co-parent the children together. Their mother lived three hours away and she came to our home to visit the kids often and she would stay the weekend at our house. It was easier for the kids because they were involved in sports and other activities and it was less expensive for her. She and I cooked Thanksgiving dinners together and hosted other family events. We also go to the movies every now and then as a family. She and I have our own friendship outside of everyone else. I take a break when she comes to visit so she cooks and cleans and I get to relax. It was trial and error and we set boundaries in the beginning. As reasonable adults we were determined to arrive at this place for the sake of our children, who have benefitted from it.

When people see me in photos with my husband's ex on Facebook I get several inbox messages asking me how I did it because they see the importance of establishing a relationship with their former spouse's ex, but so much baggage has happened over the years, they can't even fathom it.

Our daughter recently had her tonsils removed. After surgery, the doctor came out to give his report and asked "Who's mom?" We both stood up, in unison and said, "We Are!"

DUOver™ BLENDED FAMILY TIPS:

- The new spouse must have an individual relationship with each child separately and not group them all together.

- Lay ground rules on how the exes will communicate and work together to have a cohesive family.

- Always include the other parent when making decisions even though the children may live primarily with you.

CHAPTER TEN

YOUR SEX LANGUAGE DUOVER™

*Let marriage be held in honor among all, and let the marriage
bed be undefiled…*

- Heb. 13:4 (ESV)

TALKING about sex in your relationship should not be a
restricted topic. Don't assume you are providing everything
your spouse needs if you have never asked. Your goal is to satisfy each
other completely. Yes, the conversations may be awkward initially,
however, when you are more vulnerable to each other and the lines
of communication are open, sex talk will naturally become easier.
You will see how liberating it can be as you offer your spouse sugges-
tions on pleasing you as well as sharing your long-time fantasies.

*"Sex is always about emotions. Good sex is about
free emotions; bad sex is about blocked emotions."*

- Deepak Chopra

If you want to take the pressure out of the uncomfortableness,
we suggest playing the fish bowl game. Each one of you puts topics
of new things you desire or things you want done differently. Once
you have all of your ideas in the bowl, take turns picking a topic
and open the discussion. Try to start the conversation with your
immediate response of, "Definitely would, Thought about it, or
Never" and then elaborate on why. Have fun and try a few of your
"Definitely would's" while you're in the moment and keep an open
mind about your "Never's." When it comes to pleasing your partner,
practice until you get it right because ultimately you have made a
commitment to be with this person for the rest of your life. Sex
should be fun for both of you to enjoy at all times.

Of course, as time goes by you may fall into a routine so when you get a new idea you can say to your spouse, "I have something I would love for us to try." Again, keep it spontaneous and fun, with no inhibitions. As a woman, your husband will love it when you initiate sex more and have the confidence in your body to perform with the lights on. Most men who have a "good girl" may feel uneasy about sharing his desires for fear of being perceived as a freak. But if you let him know that it's OK and remind him that The Word says, "the marriage bed is undefiled," he will open up and share his sexual desires with you which will eliminate his temptation for outside influences.

Statistics show that men who help out around the house have a more active sex life because their wives are less tired. Energy level is important for a woman so the more her man contributes to the entire running of the household, the more sex her husband is going to receive. Your foreplay can start once you make eye contact with your spouse and a wink to let him know that it's time to put the kids to bed. While your spouse is reading the kids a bedtime story, you can stop by and pat him on the back or whisper in his ear to let him know that you are waiting for him in the bedroom.

MEET VIVIAN

With so much focus on looks these days, a lot of women are uncomfortable with their bodies. We all put on a few pounds as we got older and it can be more and more difficult to lose the weight and keep it off. Vivian has been divorced for five years. She has three teenagers and has recently married Phil whose primary love language is Physical Touch. Phil is madly in love with Vivian and tries his best to reassure her that he loves every part of her body even if she doesn't. We've been working with Vivian to build her confidence regarding her body image.

> **VIVIAN:** I know you both have spoken with Phil and he's said over and over that he loves me just the way I am. I really want to believe him, but I just don't love me that way.

> **KELLI:** At the end of the day, we know you want to get to the point where you do.

VIVIAN'S DUOVER™

We coached Vivian about accentuating her body with the right clothing and accessories. We provided a total makeover that helped build her confidence. She also decided to work with a personal trainer and after a few months of working out, she started feeling healthier, less lethargic, and more beautiful. Before we met Vivian, she told us how she was overtired and would insist on having sex in the dark with the covers hiding every body part. Now Vivian and Phil have sex with the lights on and even in the daytime! We have helped Vivian plan romantic evenings with Phil when he least expected it. Their marriage is now stronger than ever.

DUOver™ SEX & INTIMACY TIPS:

- Keep the spark so he stays on his toes. Since men get bored easily, you want to continuously peak his interest sexually and do the unexpected. Surprise him on a Tuesday night (don't interfere with Monday night football) when he comes home from work and let him know you sent the kids to your mother's as you are preparing dinner in sexy Victoria Secret lingerie.

- Continue to impress him by keeping your appearance up and dress for your husband like you did when you were dating. This goes both ways. A man expects his wife to look as beautiful as she did on their wedding day, while he has tacked on 30 or 40 pounds since the marriage. He may not realize that this can be unattractive to his spouse. If this has happened, suggest that you both work out together or take evening walks which offer two-fold benefits; exercising and spending quality time together.

- Learn your spouse's sex language as sexual intimacy is different from one person to the next. Just because your last partner thought something was great doesn't mean your new spouse is in agreement. Put aside your ego and continue exploring to learn each other's sex language.

TAKE IT FROM ME

I believe I have every negligee and boa from Victoria Secret, and every six-inch-stiletto from Fredericks of Hollywood. Each time I purchased something I was so excited to put them on for my husband. I never got a chance to model my new sexy investment because my husband would say, "That's nice honey, it matches really well with the carpet. Now take it off!" He preferred nothing! At first I was offended because I thought I looked as beautiful as the women in the catalogs, but he didn't care about that. As women we need to be confident with our bodies, flaws and all. It will make a big difference in your sex life. Appreciate and embrace your body. So now, when we're home alone, I cook breakfast or make a dinner in my beautiful sexy lingerie to get my money's worth!

CHAPTER ELEVEN

YOUR MAINTENANCE DUOVER™

*"We work hard to achieve that number one spot but under-
stand that you have to work even harder to keep it."*

-*The Matchmaking DUO*™

EVERLASTING FIREWORKS

CONGRATULATIONS! You've tied the knot with your one
true love. Although you've faced a few unexpected challenges,
you both still love each other and want to do everything possible to
keep the sparks alive. Is it really possible? It certainly is! The more
you make a commitment to be attentive to your spouse's needs
despite the pressures of work, children, extended family, and social
networking distractions, you'll be surprised how easy it will become
to keep the fireworks and champagne popping. You should always
find something to celebrate between you two.

*Oh yes, you will always be
My endless love…*

- *Endless Love*, *Lionel Richie*

Let's face it, if you ate the same meal every day, wore the same
clothes every day or even have the same routine every day, it can
get old fast. One woman we spoke with wore the same hairstyle for
more than 15 years. We asked her, "What are you waiting for to
change it?" "This is working fine for me. Why change it?" was her
response. We responded, "Keep it spicy!" Break the monotony and
keep him on his toes. As we mentioned in earlier chapters, men get
bored easily and they love change believe it or not. We encourage
you to change your hair color and maybe add a little to it from time
to time if he's into to that. Have your bag of *goodies* in the closet and

get ready to pull them out unexpectedly. After all, you should be doing everything in your power to keep each other happy and out of the hands of temptation!

MARRIAGE MAINTENANCE DUOVER™ TIPS:

- Make a habit being emotionally intimate with your spouse. The more you communicate, share ideas and feelings, hold hands, and provide hugs and kisses, you are building a mutual closeness that is based on comfort and trust.

- Have fun. Recreate old times when you dated or engaged in memorable activities earlier in the marriage. Pull out the photos! Plan weekend getaways to spas or other scenic and relaxing locations.

- Create intimate sexual environments in the bedroom or even a home office to surprise him. Learn your spouse's sexual needs and fantasies an act upon them often.

- Continue date nights together. Have a standing day every week that is reserved just for the two of you and mix it up between cozy nights inside and dressing up for fun events outside like a romantic dinner or night on the town.

- Make time to go out with your girlfriends once a month while he is out with the guys. Occasional time away will allow you to miss each other and look forward to the warm embrace that's waiting when you return.

- Do things with other married couples who share your interests and values. It's a way to build camaraderie and support each other's relationships.

- Keep family and friends out of the day-to-day interactions in your relationship.

TAKE IT FROM ME

When I was married, I never thought of having boundaries for my extended family. After all, we have always been very close and there for each other through some pretty high ups and very low downs. I've always been the type who enjoys their company. They also helped me adjust to being a new mom by visiting often and assisting with daily tasks. The benefits for me were two-fold; I received help and had the chance to spend time with my family regularly. The challenge with this arrangement from my husband's point of view was that he didn't feel like our home was totally ours. I've learned that it is important to have confidence in the relationship and in your role as a wife early on. Even if you don't know everything, you can research it online or ask a family member and figure it out together as a couple. Having balance is important so that you can create your own family structure and traditions, even laughing along the way at how much you didn't know but learned together.

CHAPTER TWELVE

YOUR AMICABLE BREAK-UP DUOVER

"In three words I can sum up everything I've learned about life: it goes on."

- Robert Frost

SO many women have told us that they stayed in relationships longer than they should have because they just didn't know what to say or how to do it. Then two months turned into two years, and by then they felt they had invested too much time to just leave. We suggest that in order to have the courage to leave early on, think of the *Why's* in your life. *Why* did you stay so long? Was there still something about him that kept you hanging on? *Why* do you deserve to have a quality relationship? Is it because you have worked so hard to accomplish what you have? Is it to be a good example to your children or maybe it's because you believe you're worth it? Whatever the reason, if you are truly unhappy, remind yourself of that early on. If you clearly see that his behavior and vision for the future doesn't line up with what you know you deserve, then he is not the one. It's time to make a clean break and let him go! Trust the fact that your tears today are well worth it compared to a two, three, or sometimes a ten-plus-year detour, wandering aimlessly down a road that you knew in your heart was never meant to be.

So how do you say it?

Sit him down and talk to him face-to-face so he can see your sincerity and really know you are serious. Give him the details of what you feel went wrong in the relationship and take responsibility for your part. Then let him know that it is no longer working for you and you have chosen to sever the relationship but you wish him well. Once you've had "the talk," make sure you stick to it, or else you will be limiting yourself by falling into a casual friendship with no rules and headed nowhere fast.

DUOVER™ AMICABLE BREAK-UP TIPS:

- It is important to be civil. Often times there are children involved and you want to set an example. Remind the children that the reason for the break-up is not their fault and be gentle with your words when speaking of the other parent. Remember, you both are still a part of them, so when you speak negatively of the other party, the children cannot help but internalize your words.

- As adults, his friends likely have become your friends and vice versa so you now run in the same circles. It's best not to make the entire group feel uncomfortable with details and stories of what went wrong. Stay above-board and determine which friendships should remain and which ones would be best to break off.

- Try to avoid comfortable relationships that have transitioned into "friends with benefits." Emotions are still involved and you are likely to be the one who is left holding the short end of the stick—no pun intended. This will also ward off rumors and salvage your reputation.

- Reflect on the good times and take a moment to realize what you've learned from the relationship. Celebrate the things you did well and take a moment to determine what you would work on or do better in your DUOver™ the next time around.

THE WRAP UP

TAKE TWO: Relationships are so complex yet the majority of us on the planet seek love and connection above most goals on our sometimes elaborate bucket list. So often we hear from people who make more money than some can fathom, that what's more important to them is having someone to share and celebrate achievements with, someone to support them through difficult times, and someone to experience unconditional love with, are worth more than everything they own. If they had to choose, they would give it all up to have true love.

Learn to live less inhibited and be more comfortable in YOUR own skin; not your professional title, nor your family lineage whether great or flawed. Embrace your past relationships that have not worked out as learning tools in your arsenal to make it work the next time around. Give yourself permission to have the confidence to believe and emit that light around you that says you are worthy of love, and you will surely have it. The Bible tells us that our trials are not for us, but to share with others. It wasn't easy to share our trials with the world, but if it helps someone along the way to course correct, then our tears and heartaches were not in vain.

Our prayer is that you have learned from our experiences and coaching moments to avoid similar mistakes and through our challenges you will be greater, stronger, and better equipped than ever before, as we are. We're rooting for you!!!

Here's to LOVE!!

DUO ACKNOWLEDGEMENTS

WE would like to thank some key people who have influenced us along the way. Thank you Jai Stone, our Brand Coach. We gave you our vision and you brought it to life remarkably! To Alethea Pounds, our Soror and entertainment attorney, we thank you for your legal expertise, support and being a part of our team. To the lovely ladies of Alpha Kappa Alpha Sorority, Incorporated who are doing great things and making an impact around the world, we love you!

To the amazing FGM board of advisors and staff, thank you for believing in our vision and your tireless efforts. Thank you to our FGM Glam Squad Partners across the country who create fabulous makeovers for our clients, YOU ROCK!

To our personal Celebrity Glam Team; Crystal Stokes of Crystal Stokes Photography, Roy Brasley "Bad Boy Roy" our make-up artist, Tracy Riggs of Tracy Riggs Salon, Shandy Massey of Halo Salon, Deana Timpanaro of The House of Dilarantz. Thank you for making us look and feel beautiful.

To our Essence Love & Relationship family, you provided an amazing platform for us to share our gifts with the masses and we thank you. To our awesome clients, thank you for your support and trusting us to assist you in your journey. To all of our readers, social media followers, and colleagues worldwide, we enjoy engaging with you as you keep us on our toes and striving to learn and do more.

Thank you. And finally, to Kim Rouse our book coach, words cannot express our gratitude. We came to you with two voices, two writing styles, and two different personalities and you designed a strategy to make it work…Sheer Genius!

TO SCHEDULE SPEAKING ENGAGEMENTS OR
DUOVER™ WORKSHOPS, contact us at

speaking@fgmatch.com

IF YOU'RE READY FOR YOUR DUOVER™

OR TO BECOME A CLIENT, contact us at
duovers@fgmatch.com

notes

notes

notes

notes

notes

notes

notes

notes

notes

notes

notes

CPSIA information can be obtained
at www.ICGtesting.com
Printed in the USA
BVOW11s0109080617
486348BV00007B/35/P